Food
from an Irish garden

Food

from an Irish garden

THE GOOD LIFE AT HUNTERS LODGE

FIONA DILLON

ORPEN PRESS

Orpen Press
Lonsdale House
Avoca Avenue
Blackrock
Co. Dublin
Ireland

e-mail: info@orpenpress.com
www.orpenpress.com

ISBN: 978-1-909518-99-5

For Eamonn
You are the measure of my dreams.

Acknowledgements

First and foremost, huge thanks and buckets of love to my husband, Eamonn, and my children, Joe, Kate, Ellie and Ruth, who were more than happy for me to abandon all domestic goddess duties to write this book. Thank you for the encouragement, for believing in me and for having the patience of saints during the many photo shoots you have all endured over the past few months (except Joe, who ran a mile every time he saw my camera!).

When Orpen Press came knocking on my door inviting me to write this book it really was a dream come true, and it has been such a pleasure to work with them. Particular thanks to my fabulous editor, Jennifer Thompson, who has been nothing but kind, considerate and supportive throughout this whirlwind year. I'm not sure we were supposed to have so much fun, but we did.

I really enjoyed the trips down memory lane with my parents, Joe and Céline Molloy, while writing this book. How fortunate I am to have been reared with an ingrained understanding of where good food comes from. We have enjoyed many a chat about my grandmothers during the writing of this book. Such memories are indeed treasures.

Thanks also to my mother-in-law, Lesley Dillon, the lady who showed me how to make jam many years ago and who now shares her baking secrets with my girls.

To my food blogging friends too numerous to mention – your support has been tremendous, and I really appreciate all the words of encouragement.

Thanks also to my blog readers who follow the ups and downs of life at Hunters Lodge and stay with me through the highs and lows. I love and appreciate your company.

To my friends Michéle and Derek Hanley who open their garden to me whenever I need to 'rob' produce. Thanks for the apples and the raspberries. You know I will repay you in sausages!

Thanks also to Tom and Mary Nolan, who are always on hand to help me. Whether it's a stranded child, feed for the pigs or a pot of home-made marmalade, their support is endless, as is my gratitude.

Beekeeping continues to be a huge learning curve, made so much easier with the advice and guidance of one of Ireland's best beekeepers, John Blanche. He is worth his weight in liquid gold!

Training with Kilkenny photographer Pat Shortall gave me the confidence to shoot the photographs for this book myself. Thank you Pat for putting up with the most inquisitive student you have ever had, and thank you also for taking the photos of me in this book.

Thanks also to my friends and colleagues in the world of radio broadcasting who have allowed me to spread my back-to-basics message with listeners, and, in particular, thanks to those who have entrusted me with my own radio show. Spreading the word about traditional food values will never fall on deaf ears.

Thank you,
Fiona xx

Contents

Preface

I MAY HAVE BEEN BORN in County Offaly and had all my schooling in County Galway, but I was always a bit of a townie at heart. My father, from Ferbane in County Offaly, and my mother, from Glenageary in County Dublin, started their married life in the big smoke, but a new job opportunity for my father meant a return to country life for my parents. By the time I was finished my Leaving Cert, I was ready for a new adventure. I quickly settled into life in Dublin. My love affair with our capital city had begun many years beforehand during sunshiny summers spent with my grandmother in Glenageary. To this day, however, my father still says to me, 'Never forget you're a bog woman', something of which I am quite proud.

The years passed, I met Eamonn, the love of my life, and our children arrived. We had a lovely home in the city, happy children, a successful business and a property portfolio. I thought the only reason we would ever leave our beloved home in Ballsbridge would be to move to a bigger house to accommodate our ever-expanding family. Well, I got that wrong!

The children were growing up and the prospect of living in the country started to appeal more and more. Eamonn and I were also looking for our next challenge. One day in 1998 we had a picnic with the children in fields of barley in Killerig, County Carlow. This land had been in Eamonn's family for some time, and, on that sunny day, the decision was made. The following year we moved lock, stock and barrel to Hunters Lodge in Ballintrane, County Carlow, a home that was to become our refuge in the ensuing years.

I have to say straight off that I had absolutely no *real* experience of living in the countryside. My move from Ballsbridge to Ballintrane was, at the very least, a slight culture shock. All of a sudden traffic jams were non-existent. Birds sang happily in the trees. The blackest night skies seemed to be bursting with a million stars – a far cry from the beeping horns, sirens, tailbacks and crowds we had lived with in Dublin. I was hooked immediately. Luckily for me, my totally citified children were as enamoured as I was, thanks in no small part to the fact that they now had an acre of gardens in which they could run wild.

Sound idyllic? Well, yes, it was, except for one small matter: Eamonn and I had arrived in Carlow to work on a new business, not to get back to basics in the country. Over the next seven years we transformed those barley fields in which we had picnicked into an 18-hole championship golf course, four-star hotel, spa and clubhouse. And we were burnt out.

Our life had quickly become a pattern of work, children and sleep, work, children and sleep. Between us, Eamonn and I were working up to eighteen hours a day, six or seven days a week. Ridiculous! And how the years were flying by (during this time our fourth child was born). We had never known pressure like it. Our responsibilities were enormous, the demands on our time were relentless, and the financial pressure was unimaginable. To this day I find it hard to think about all the sleepless nights and the worry that was permanently etched in my naturally easygoing husband's eyes. I try not to dwell on how cruel and ruthless people can be towards each other in the world of business. Having said that, the experience taught me a lot about values, and it is one of the reasons I am so content today. If my husband and children are healthy and happy, there's nothing much that can stress me these days.

By 2008 we had walked away from the corporate world without a penny between us. But after years of being pulled every which way, we knew that our priority going forward had to be our family. We were willing to live on nothing just to have some sort of 'normal' family life. Eamonn knew he wanted once again to have his own small business, one which would allow him to have plenty of family time. And I knew I wanted nothing more than to immerse myself in family life: cooking, baking, gardening, housework …. There was only one minor problem: I was absolutely rubbish at all those things!

During my working years, I had hired a nanny and then a housekeeper. At any given time I knew the house was clean and the children were well fed and never short on love or attention. But now the time had come for me to do it all myself. I can well understand how the prospect of domestic bliss could send many a woman fleeing back to the corporate world, but I do love a challenge.

I made myself a promise: if I was going to cook dinners, they were going to be the finest dinners my family could eat. And if I wasn't going to be going out into the workplace and earning a living it was now my job to produce those family meals as economically as possible. I already kept a few chickens and, with an acre of space at my disposal, I figured why not grow some food as well?

It's true that no plan is straightforward, but finding myself seriously ill in hospital in January 2009 certainly wasn't on the agenda. The diagnosis? Graves Disease, an auto-immune disease brought on by years of relentless stress. No surprise there then. That's when I made a promise to myself I will die of anything but stress. Anything!

I left hospital revitalised and more determined than ever to grow my own food. I attended organic vegetable growing courses in the nearby village of Ballon, and they transformed my life. It may sound a little dramatic, but it's true. I was so fortunate to have the most wonderful tutor (a Carlow woman named Liz Brown) and, to this day, she remains my hero. She got me on the right path. I went from knowing nothing to having no fear when it comes to growing food. What's the worst that can happen? I now had chickens for eggs and fantastic fresh vegetables. In no time, soft fruits, apple trees, pigs, turkeys and bees were added. My back-to-basics journey had begun. Life in the garden got really exciting, and the kitchen became my favourite room in the house.

☺ HUNTERS LODGE LIVING – THE BLOG ☝

Have I mentioned that all my children were All-Ireland Competitive Ballroom Champions at one point or another between 2006 and 2011? The reason I'm telling you (very proud

mama!) is because the people involved in that circuit (friends, fellow parents, competitors, etc.) witnessed my transformation from business woman to 'Barbara Good'. This, coupled with constant questions from my family, prompted me to start a blog in May 2010. I had always liked to write and, this way, my family and friends could also see what I was up to. Best of all, I had an online diary to refer back to during the growing year.

What I didn't foresee were the other side effects of blogging. Within a few months of starting my blog, I was asked to feature in *Irish Country Living* (the *Irish Farmers Journal* supplement). For a (city) girl like me, this was just crazy, and the response was even crazier. Nowadays, I write in their stand-alone glossy magazine, *Irish Country* – something I am very proud of.

But other opportunities arose from blogging. I was invited to do a guest slot on a local radio station, and I now present my own show on Community Radio Kilkenny City. I love the medium of radio and, back in 2012, I had the opportunity to take myself to college to do some PR and media studies. During this time I also became a certified trainer so I could show others how they, too, can get back to basics. The opportunities that have arisen from blogging have been endless and really good fun. Film crews and radio shows have recorded here at Hunters Lodge, I've made some amazing friends, and we Dillons are having a ball! But the most exciting point so far was, without doubt, being approached to write this book.

No experience is required to recreate our back-to-basics life at Hunters Lodge in your own home. If I can do it, anyone can. Believe me, my **KISS** (Keep It Simple Silly) motto has stood me in good stead throughout the years. Nobody needs added complications in their life.

And on the off-chance you may be thinking that over the years I transformed into an all-singing, all-dancing Irish version of Martha Stewart, I must point out that I have *never* gotten to grips with the housework element of my plan!

Fiona Dillon
Hunters Lodge, Ballintrane, County Carlow
August 2013

Life at Hunters Lodge

🍎 FAMILY VALUES 🧅

*I*T MIGHT BE the only positive, but this recession has definitely brought with it a yearning to return to the traditional ways of feeding families with the most nutritious and wholesome food, and at the least expense. A sense of nostalgia tinges so many thoughts and conversations nowadays – not for Celtic Tiger times, but for our grandmothers' time. A time when mothers all over the country had very little money, but they donned their apron every morning and proceeded to bake and cook mouth-watering food from home-grown and home-reared produce.

It is not that long ago that many families – from the most central house in Dublin to the most rural smallholding – kept a pig and chickens in their yard. Even in the toughest of times, they had eggs, chicken, pork and bacon to eat. They baked bread and made butter. If they had space, they sowed potatoes and vegetables. They were healthy. Back then, obesity hadn't been heard of. I'm only too well aware of the time and space constraints that exist nowadays, but these constraints don't stop people longing to rear their children with the food values of yesteryear.

I say it time and time again that one of the most important jobs I do is teach my children about where their food comes from. With the onslaught of more and more supermarkets and hyper-markets, children are becoming increasingly removed from the origins of their food. It's a worrying trend, but one that can easily be rectified if everyone does a little bit. You need no more than a packet of seeds and a windowsill to start teaching your children about growing food, and those lessons will stay with them for the rest of their lives. Nowadays, we also have the wonderful benefit of modern appliances, making it easier and less time-consuming to integrate traditional food values into our lives.

That's how we do things at Hunters Lodge, and in this book I share all our traditional lifestyle ideas, tips and recipes to help you and your family get back to basics, just like our foremothers and forefathers.

🍎 HUNTERS LODGE 🍐

Our house is called Hunters Lodge because, over one hundred years ago, a little lodge stood here, and it was known as a place where hunters in the area could stop and rest. In fact, when we bought the house back in 1999, the deeds contained a clause that allowed any 'hunter' in the area to rest here.

These days, the house is pretty modern, with all the usual amenities. It's probably just like your house. I'd love to tell you about the huge Aga in my country farmhouse kitchen, but I have neither the cooker nor the kitchen to match. Ours is a typical busy home, always filled with the hustle and bustle of people coming and going. Yet, for whatever reason, there's a wonderful sense of nostalgia here. A nod to bygone traditions can be found in every corner of the house and garden.

Perhaps it's the smell of bread baking in the kitchen or the happy chickens foraging in the garden that give it a sense of a bygone era. Or maybe it's the happy little dog that greets you on arrival (unless you're Tony the postman!), or the heady smell of freshly cut grass that envelops you as you drive through the gate. One thing I know for sure is that wherever I live in the world, be it a remote island or a noisy city, I know it's possible to recreate some of the wonderful food traditions of my grandmothers' time. And while I suspect there aren't too many hunters wandering out there today, they are still most welcome to stop and rest at Hunters Lodge.

🍎 MY LARDER 🍎

The larder at Hunters Lodge is well stocked year round. We have a plentiful supply of eggs (chicken, duck, quail and goose) and, every spring, we rear broiler chickens for the table. We also rear our own turkey for Christmas. Every year we grow our own potatoes (you won't believe how easy it is), and it has been years since I've bought garlic or shallots in the supermarket, such is our yearly yield. Onions, leeks, beetroot and cabbage are some of our kitchen-garden staples, while fresh peas, tomatoes, cucumbers, herbs and salads adorn our plates throughout the summer. Two pigs give us a year-round supply of pork and bacon, and five beehives provide us with plenty of honey, with enough left over for family and friends. Apple trees are dotted throughout the garden, and there's nothing nicer than popping outside to collect apples for an apple tart. We have a plentiful supply of rhubarb – nobody leaves Hunters Lodge without a bunch – and we grow a variety of soft fruits. Ice cream and jams made from home-grown fresh strawberries and raspberries are a pure joy to eat. But whether its gooseberries and redcurrants or carrots and broad beans that you want to grow, here's my golden rule:

> Only grow food that you enjoy eating.

If you and your family don't enjoy cabbage, then there is no point in having a dozen of the finest heads of cabbage in your garden simply because you find it easy to grow. Grow what you like to eat, and you can't go wrong. Having said that, don't get too boring either – experiment with something new every year.

🍎 YOUR HEALTH IS YOUR WEALTH 🍎

We six Dillons enjoy very good health. We don't take vitamins or supplements; we get more than enough goodness from the food that we eat. Now don't worry, I'm not going to start ranting about fast food, genetically modified (GM) foods or additives in foods. It's up to each of us to make our own informed decisions about what to feed ourselves and our families. Life is all about balance, after all, and I would be lying if I said I didn't enjoy a takeaway occasionally – but certainly not every night! You know what they say, 'everything in moderation'.

The more I grow and rear my own food, the more interested I've become in natural remedies to cure common ailments. Believe it or not, these remedies not only work for me and my family but for my chickens as well. Honey, garlic, rosehip syrup – their healing properties are well documented, and later in this book I'll show you how I use them.

🍎 SIZE DOESN'T MATTER 🍎

Time and time again people say to me, 'I'd love to visit your farm', or 'your farm sounds great.' What farm? I don't have a farm. I don't even have a smallholding. I have a garden. Having a decent-sized garden does allow me to raise chickens, geese and pigs, but you don't need an enormous garden to dip into this book or take the first steps towards a simpler lifestyle.

One of my best friends bought an apartment some years back, and we had great fun planning all the food he could grow on his balcony and windowsills. Herbs, tomatoes, cucumbers, salads, potatoes and strawberries were all possible. Not bad! A standard garden will more than accommodate a small chicken coop, raised beds and fruit bushes. And what's to stop you having a potato bag on your patio? Herbs and salads can be grown in the smallest of spaces, and hanging baskets brimming with tomatoes or strawberries make a welcome addition to any balcony or porch.

The possibilities are endless, and each chapter will have lots of ideas for you to consider. If you can't grow the recipe ingredients yourself right now, they are all easily available at local markets. Some of my recipes cost almost nothing: a healthy walk in the countryside is all that is required to pick up the ingredients. So don't let size be an issue. Work with what you have and, in no time at all, you'll be enjoying your own harvests.

> The size you have to work with is the size you have to work with, be it big or small. The size of your growing space can be your excuse for not doing anything or the reason that you grow your own food – it's up to you.

☺ THE TIME IS RIPE ☺

'I don't have the time' is a common reason people give for not growing their own food. With the pace of modern life forcing many of us to spread ourselves too thinly, it's no wonder we often feel there just aren't enough hours in the day. Work, children, friends, family, after-school activities – not to mention cooking, cleaning, laundry, cutting the grass … I could go on and on. How could you possibly find the time to grow and rear your own food on top of all your other weekly tasks? Here's how:

> One step at a time.

Setting yourself small goals or tasks will help make growing your own food much easier. This could mean buying a packet of seeds, a tomato plant or constructing your first raised bed. Start with a small project that doesn't become a chore, but rather a

relaxing hobby. When people attend classes here at Hunters Lodge I always caution them about jumping in head first when I see their faces lighting up with enthusiasm. It's abundantly clear that they're very excited to go home and get started. And that's great but, believe me, if you go home and decide to dig six vegetable beds the next day, you'll tire quickly and the novelty will wear off just as quickly. Slowly does it.

Growing and rearing food should be a pleasant way of life and not another chore to add to your weekly to-do list.

Think about how much time you can commit before you start. It doesn't need to be a lot of time, but it should be a time in your week that is both relaxing and enjoyable.

What if you can't commit to growing and rearing right now? Or maybe you don't have a garden? Cupboards can still be filled with pots of home-made goodness, made at your leisure. What's to stop you filling your home with the smell of freshly baked scones, filling your windowsills with herbs or making a pot of jam for your neighbour? Lots of visitors to Hunters Lodge don't have large gardens but, by the end of their visit, they're armed with ideas and recipes to recreate a farmhouse kitchen larder in their own home. Keep reading and you will be too.

A COSTLY EXERCISE?

Some time ago I recorded a piece here at Hunters Lodge for a well-known RTÉ radio programme. My phone went crazy after the programme aired with people wanting to know how they could recreate our lifestyle, but one call really stuck out in my mind. The conversation started off like a lot of the others: 'I have a few acres and I want to do what you're doing.' I was speaking with a lovely gentleman who was obviously keen to get started on his own self-sufficiency project. His next question was 'How much?' I presumed he meant to attend one of my classes, but what he actually wanted to know was roughly how much it would cost to transform his land into a self-sufficient plot. I had never actually considered this before. I hadn't even thought about a budget when I started out. To me, the whole point of becoming more self-sufficient was to save money, not spend it. I was a stay-at-home mum with four children. Granted, I was very lucky that my husband's new business was thriving but, in my mind, my job was to feed my family with the best of ingredients and as economically as possible. I certainly wasn't going to run out and buy new chicken coops and raised beds and glasshouses.

Instead I **reuse and recycle**. I have a very simple philosophy when it comes to spending money on new equipment: how many eggs do I have to sell to afford the item? Let me tell you, if you are selling half a dozen eggs for €2 it very quickly puts the cost of greenhouses and the like into perspective. This has been an invaluable lesson for my children, who sell eggs at the gate during the summer months. So, my reply to that gentleman? This exercise can be as costly or as cost-effective as you make it. If your budget only allows for a packet of seeds, start with that. If you can afford wire for a chicken run, great! Nothing about this lifestyle should cause you stress – financially or otherwise. The whole idea is to live a simpler lifestyle with traditional food values.

We make our own chicken coops with recycled wood, our glasshouse is made with recycled glass doors, and our first pig run was made with old pallets. When I say 'we make', I actually mean Eamonn makes them. I come up with the ideas and he brings them to life. Hey, it works for us!

If you want to buy yourself a little greenhouse to get started, by all means go ahead. You'll get hours and hours of pleasure from it (especially if you put in a comfy chair), and you will absolutely reap great rewards. But don't worry if you can't afford this luxury; it's not necessary. I started off growing my seedlings on windowsills all over the house – and so can you. The same goes for a chicken coop. There are some amazing Irish hand-crafted coops on the market, but you can always make your own if you want to. You decide what you want to spend. And start keeping egg cartons, toilet-roll inserts and yoghurt cartons; they'll come in very handy.

SELF-SUFFICIENT?

Here at Hunters Lodge we are a pretty ordinary two-parent, four-child family. Our lives are probably pretty similar to yours: work, school runs, after-school activities, music, ballet, matches – sound familiar? I wonder sometimes whether the term 'self-sufficient' really applies to us at all. We're not living 'off the grid'. We have electricity and running water, and we go to the supermarket and butchers to supplement the foods that we grow and rear ourselves. So maybe in the strictest terms we're not self-sufficient. But what is food self-sufficiency if it's not growing your own fruit and vegetables and rearing your own meat? If we can serve meat, potatoes and vegetables with a plot-to-plate distance of 100 feet, well, that's self-sufficient enough for us. Couple that with our love of uncomplicated recipes packed with flavour (many of them popular Irish dishes from a bygone era) and we've got ourselves a simple back-to-basics lifestyle. And we love it!

☺ EATING MEAT ☺

People who visit Hunters Lodge are often surprised to see two geese strolling contentedly around the garden. These are my pets. Mahatma Gander and Willow Goose are as much a part of our family as our little dog Pippi is. While geese generally don't have a reputation for placidity, Mahatma is so gentle that he happily eats out of my hand. Having said that, it is true that geese make excellent 'guard dogs', and they alert me to any visitors approaching my door by screeching very loudly. In the middle of the night, this screeching has also alerted us to the fact that there's a fox in the garden. If you have a pet that you love, then you'll know exactly how I feel about my gander. Needless to say, the one thing we don't rear for the table is goose.

We do raise chickens and pigs for consumption, however. We kept chickens for ten years before we were ready to rear birds for the table. It is a big jump from keeping chickens for eggs to keeping chickens with the intention of using them for food. (For more details on raising chickens, see Chapter 2.) While many people applaud my efforts to rear my own meat, there have been those who have suggested that I'm cruel and heartless to do this. Nothing could be further from the truth. We are not vegetarians. We enjoy meat. And we never have to wonder or worry about where our meat comes from or what the animals were fed. The animals we rear for the table have the best of food, love and attention. We have the utmost respect for them. It's very easy to pop into the supermarket and pick up some pork chops, not thinking for one second about the life the animal might have had. It's certainly a lot easier than rearing a pig for six months and enduring the heartache of bringing it to slaughter. But that is my choice. I choose to give my family the best food that I can provide. Believe me, the animals reared at Hunters Lodge are the lucky ones. It's not for everybody, but it works for us.

For Eamonn and me, one of our greatest pleasures is giving half a dozen rashers to friends and family. From anyone over a certain age, the feedback is always the same: they were 'real' rashers, with the taste and thickness evoking memories of childhood Sunday breakfasts. And our children get to enjoy this same quality, just like we did as youngsters.

FOOD THROUGH THE SEASONS

Growing food is a year-round activity, and at Hunters Lodge there is always something happening in the garden or in the kitchen.

STARTING THE DAY

I start each day in the garden by feeding the hens, ducks, geese and quail. If it's during the summer months, I also feed the pigs. If it's winter, I feed the turkeys. Then I collect the eggs. I usually collect the eggs first thing in the morning, but I also like to take a wander in the late afternoon and collect the last of the day's eggs. I find this very therapeutic.

IN THE KITCHEN

Baking bread happens every week. Traditional Irish soda bread and yeast-free brown bread are our staples. They are simple and quick to make, and they taste great. I can still remember my grandmother Isabella taking soda bread out of the Aga on a Sunday afternoon. The smell and the taste were like nothing else on earth. Now, I recreate this wonderful memory for my children.

I have included not only our own family-favourite recipes in this book but also the recipes that have had the most appeal to my blog readers over the past few years. Whether it's a Madeira cake for visitors or baked eggs for Sunday brunch, I hope you enjoy them as much as we do. For these and other recipes see Chapter 6.

SPRING HAS SPRUNG – THE NOBLE SPUD

Are we not a nation of potato lovers? The Italians have their pasta – we have our spuds. I think the first time I harvested potatoes was the first time I felt like a truly 'grown-up' gardener. And it was so easy!

Once the first snowdrops appear it's time to start thinking about chitting potatoes. This is the process of allowing shoots to grow on your potatoes before you plant them. I love planning what varieties I'm going to sow. This sparks great debate with family and friends, who all have their own favourites. Who likes waxy spuds? Who likes floury spuds? One thing I know for sure is that every year I must have King Edwards. I absolutely adore them. We actually call them King Eamonns here in honour of the master of the house.

When it comes to growing potatoes, some years are great, and other years blight gets the better of us, but nothing stops us giving it a go every year. One of the things visitors love to see here is how we reuse coal sacks to grow our early potatoes. In Chapter 4, I'll show you exactly how you can do this too.

SUMMER SENSATIONS – BEE HAPPY

The summer sees the arrival of soft fruits, bringing with it jam- and ice-cream-making season. What could be nicer than home-made strawberry jam on top of the freshest soda bread? Ah, but you would need real butter, so why not make that too? Butter is really easy to make, and in Chapter 6 I'll show you how.

If the weather is any way fine, we like to barbeque and eat outdoors as often as possible. I survive the long winter months dreaming of balmy summer evenings with that unmistakeable smell of the barbeque. A table brimming with home-grown salads, baby potatoes and freshly baked breads just needs to be surrounded by family and friends!

By the end of the summer it's time to harvest the honey. Since we started beekeeping we have always been fortunate enough to yield enough honey to keep us self-sufficient from year to year. We use it for our home-made granola, drizzled on fresh bread as an afternoon treat and added to yoghurt to make a lovely topping for fresh fruit. No sore throat stands a chance of getting the better of us when we're armed with a teaspoon of honey from our own garden. It is a true superfood and one that we are privileged to have.

Beekeeping has become quite popular nowadays, and it's true we need all the beekeepers we can get (see Chapter 7 for more details on beekeeping). I had never thought about keeping bees until some years ago I was at a local St Patrick's Day parade and a float went by with the name and number of a nearby beekeeping association. The rest, as they say, is history. Beekeeping is a huge learning curve, and I'm so fortunate that

Eamonn is really passionate about the welfare of our bees. It is not something to be undertaken lightly, but the rewards are enormous. When you are working with bees, time seems to stand still, and the hours pass away unnoticed. Bees are amazing creatures to whom we owe so much.

AUTUMN HARVEST – FORAGED FEASTS

As autumn descends and the leaves start to fall, foraging season is upon us. Now we can look forward to gathering rosehips, sloes, crab apples and blackberries (see Chapter 8). A walk in the countryside is all that's required to gather this food. It is at this time of year that I make hedgerow jams, sloe gin for Christmas and rosehip syrup to boost our vitamin C levels throughout the dark winter.

Autumn throws out the most amazing colours, colours you won't find at any other time of the year, and they are truly special. Autumn raspberries fruit right into October. We pick them daily and store them in the freezer. On frosty January mornings they make a welcome reappearance atop stacks of home-made pancakes.

By November, when the beehives are settled all snug and tight against the cold, we sow our garlic and onions for the following year. No matter how low the temperatures dip, those little shoots will appear without fail in the spring. By this time, the pigs will be gone, only to be replaced with our turkey for Christmas Day (see Chapter 7 for details on raising turkeys). On Christmas Day itself, it always gives me enormous pleasure to pop down to the vegetable garden to pick sprouts for dinner. I never grow too many. Why? Yes, you've guessed it – I'm the only one who likes them. But throughout the year other vegetables have been picked and frozen to be brought out now for that special dinner.

And that's how it goes. In every month of every season one thing starts and another thing ends. No month is boring, and there's no month that doesn't give us food. In many ways it's simple and uncomplicated, but the simplicity brings with it such quality of life.

One day many years ago I recall being out in the garden as the rain poured down and my wellies squelched in the muck. It struck me that when I was enduring those same weather conditions in my previous life, I would have been worried that my shoes would be destroyed, my suit would get wet, my make-up would be ruined and, the ultimate horror, my hair would go frizzy! But on that day in the garden I just grinned – none of that mattered anymore, and I truly knew the meaning of the word 'freedom'.

This book is not meant to be a step-by-step guide to fruit and vegetable gardening. There are plenty of manuals and guidebooks out there that will cover topics like soil types and diseases. What I want to show you is that even though our lives might be busier than ever, it is still possible to grow some of your own food and enjoy great riches from your garden. I am sharing our lifestyle with you. If you have any desire to live more sustainably or self-sufficiently, my advice and tips will set you on that journey and help you discover the joy of having real food on your plate.

I grow all my food as organically as possible. I don't use chemicals or artificial fertilizers. I use home-made garlic sprays as insect repellents, and comfrey and nettle teas as fertilizers (see Chapter 3). This is my choice. Because organic produce is more expensive in supermarkets, I presumed it would cost more to grow. I was wrong. If anything, organic growing is easier. You leave nature alone. You don't have the expense of chemicals and sprays. Areas in the garden that I might have thought were in need of tidying up years ago are now left overgrown with wildflowers for the butterflies and bees. I love to see areas of wilderness in the garden; it's as nature intended. It also means I don't have the stress of ensuring all the garden borders are neat and tidy. I really do like the way nature thinks!

As you flick through the following chapters, you will notice the word 'home' meandering through the pages: home-grown, home-reared and home-made. Taking home-grown produce and transforming it into simple nutritious food for your loved ones will fill you with joy. But food in all forms has the ability to evoke powerful memories from your past. Growing my own food and using ingredients and recipes that my grandmothers made throws me back to warm sunny days with my grandmothers, Isabella and Stella. And now those same home-grown, home-made breads and dinners are creating what I am sure will be warm and comforting memories for my own children – long into the future.

Our Feathered Friends –
A Beginner's Guide to Keeping Chickens

2

WHEN WE DECIDED to move to the country, one of the first things I thought was that we should keep chickens. For me it made perfect sense. How could you have the whole country-life experience without a cock-a-doodle-doo to wake you up in the morning? I had no experience of keeping chickens, but I figured if generations before me had managed it, then so would I. This really made Dad laugh. Mum, on the other hand, knew that if I had the idea in my head, then it was going to happen. It continues to be the best decision I ever made.

At that time, poultry keeping hadn't regained its popularity, so there was little guidance available. I decided not to let that deter me. I bought a chicken book online and, with my husband building a chicken coop, my dream became a reality.

I was working crazy hours every day back then, but, believe it or not, those chickens helped me keep my sanity. Never mind having a supply of the most fantastic fresh eggs, the chickens became my stress-free zone. Those few minutes a day away from all the stresses and strains proved to be invaluable to me, but also to us as a family. I'm not sure there could be a nicer hobby for all the family than keeping chickens. I have never met a child who doesn't like to collect eggs. With a little planning you too could be collecting your own fresh eggs every day. Poultry keepers never forget the day they collected their first eggs. We were very nearly tempted to put a shop-bought egg in the nest, such was the children's excitement, but we just waited for nature to take its course. The first egg was eventually laid, and we never looked back.

I'm sure you're only too well aware, but whenever you come up with an idea there will always be people to tell you why you shouldn't proceed with it. Naturally enough, my plan to keep chickens was met with a certain amount of negativity, always from people who didn't actually keep chickens. The smell would be vile and they would attract vermin, they said. Anyway, weren't eggs cheap enough in the supermarket? I didn't know what sounded worse: the possibility of a bad smell hanging around the garden or supermarket eggs from poor battery hens. Like most things I do, I decided I would learn the hard way and just do it. After all, if you didn't wash your dog, it would smell. And we all know what a fish bowl smells like if it's not cleaned out. Likewise, a dirty coop wouldn't be pleasant, so I figured I would just keep it clean. A little basic hygiene goes a long way.

As for the chickens attracting vermin, even in the city there's no avoiding them. Surely, if I didn't give these creatures an endless supply of free food, they would have no reason to pay any special attention to my garden? I thought that if I just stored the chickens' food correctly, vermin would have no access to it and wouldn't bother hanging around. This has proven to be true over the years. So, I carried on regardless. Now I cannot remember the last time I bought eggs.

In this chapter I'll show you how to get started on the road to successfully keeping chickens. At my classes, I'm asked the same questions over and over again, and here you'll find the answers to them all. Whenever I write an article about starting with chickens for a magazine or a blog, the information never really changes. Over the years I've learned from trial and error. I've found shortcuts and learned the hard way what works best. The information in this chapter is what I think you should know to help you get started. It continues to work for me, and there's no reason why it won't work for you.

Before I go any further, let me just clarify something. The word 'chickens' refers to both males and females. Cockerels (or roosters) are the males, and when I mention hens I'm referring to the little ladies that lay those delicious eggs.

🍎 WHY DO YOU WANT TO KEEP CHICKENS? 🐣

You may want to keep chickens for a variety of reasons, the most common and obvious being for a supply of fresh eggs. Some people keep chickens as pets, others see the fertilizer they provide as second to none, and yet more people want to raise chickens for meat. Whatever the reason, keeping a few chickens seems to go hand in hand with a more self-sufficient lifestyle, and it has become a starting point for many people.

If you are considering getting some chickens, ask yourself the following questions before you go any further:

🐤 Can you provide safe and secure shelter for the chickens?
🐤 Can you provide a continuous supply of fresh food and water?
🐤 Can you commit time for general husbandry – cleaning the coop, worming, etc.?

If you answered 'yes', 'yes' and 'yes' – let's get started!

WHERE DO I START?

Consider very carefully the amount of space you have for your chickens. Do you plan to have them free-ranging in the garden or will they be confined to a chicken run? It may sound idyllic to have your chickens strolling around your garden, but you must consider the following:

PREDATORS

I'm sure you're thinking foxes and mink here, but some domesticated animals like dogs and cats can also pose a threat to chickens. Safe housing and secure runs are vital if you want to protect your flock, particularly at night.

FLOWER AND VEGETABLE BEDS

Chickens like nothing better than freshly dug soil. They'll happily join you as you dig your flower bed and scratch away for hours. Great if you are prepping a bed for sowing vegetables. Not so great if you've just planted flower bulbs. Established, full beds won't be a problem, but if you have an area of soil between your plants/shrubs, your chickens might like to use it as a dust bath (I'll explain that one later).

If you are determined to let your chickens free-range in the garden, then some well-thought-out netting/fencing will protect any vulnerable flower and vegetable beds. If you decide not to let your chickens roam free in the garden, they will be happy to scratch around in an adequately-sized chicken run.

CHICKEN COOPS AND RUNS

There are some incredible chicken coops on the market at the moment: bespoke, hand-crafted coops that would make an attractive addition to any garden, but they come with a handsome price tag. However, it's not difficult to find an adequate chicken coop to suit almost every budget. Even made-to-measure coops can be quite affordable. And if you're into DIY, there's no end of coop designs available on the Internet free of charge.

Chicken Coop Basics

Whether coops are built or bought, they should all be designed to provide the same thing: a dry, well-ventilated house with a roost and one or more nest boxes. You should provide a minimum of 2 square feet per hen. This will help you decide on the number of chickens you can keep, and the size of coop that you need.

A good chicken coop should:

- Be dry with good ventilation
- Have a roosting area
- Have one or more nest boxes
- Allow at least 2 square feet per chicken
- Provide easy access to all areas for cleaning
- Have secure access in and out of the coop

Chicken coops are usually situated inside a run. If space is an issue, you can choose to attach a small run to your coop. This is suitable only for those thinking of keeping no more than a few hens.

If you buy/build a coop with a run attached, it should be possible to move the structure quite easily (by attaching wheels), allowing your chickens access to fresh grass every few days.

If you are building a run in your garden, take the following into consideration:

- If your chickens won't be free-ranging in the garden, this will be their foraging area, so make it as big as you can.
- Use the strongest chicken wire you can afford. This will help keep out predators.
- Be sure to bury the wire 18 inches into the ground to prevent unwanted visitors digging their way into your run.
- Over time, the grass in your run will wear away. After heavy rain your run will quickly turn mucky. Chickens don't like to have wet feet. You can use untreated woodchips or suitable gravel on the ground to prevent a smell and a build-up of organisms that may lead to disease. I layer the ground with straw throughout the winter and

remove it to the compost area in spring. This works for me because my birds leave the run in the mornings to free-range in the garden throughout the day.

🍎 KNOW YOUR CHICKENS 🍐

LARGE FOWL

These are standard pure-breed chickens, such as Light Sussex, Rhode Island Reds and Orpingtons. They lay a good size egg of varying colours, depending on the breed.

BANTAMS

Bantams are a much smaller bird than a regular chicken. They lay a smaller egg but are an ideal choice if space is very limited. Being smaller, they also eat much less. Some bantams (like Silkies and Pekins) often become pets because of their wonderfully docile nature. A lot of bantam varieties can be quite broody, making them ideal if you intend to hatch out your own chicks.

HYBRIDS

Hybrid hens, a cross between two pure-bred birds, make excellent layers. The broody instinct is almost completely bred out of them, making them a good choice if you don't intend to hatch chicks.

BROILERS

Broiler chickens are reared solely for the table. Modern broilers have lost a lot of their foraging instincts, but certain breeds, like Wessex Supreme, will still forage if allowed to free-range. Our broilers free-range with our other birds.

WHAT'S RIGHT FOR ME?

There's a huge variety to choose from when it comes to buying your chickens. If you want a very dark egg, choose a breed like Marans or Wellsummers. If you prefer a blue–green egg, choose a Cream Legbar or an Araucana. If you're looking for a broody breed, Silkies (bantams), Light Sussex and Orpingtons are good options.

TO BROOD OR NOT TO BROOD?

Your hen will lay eggs whether you have a cockerel or not. She's a hen, that's what she does. However, without a cockerel, your hen cannot lay a fertilized egg. This is not a problem if you are simply keeping hens so that you can eat their eggs. However, if you would like to hatch chicks, Mr Cockerel will have to visit your ladies to ensure that the eggs are fertilized.

> You do not need a cockerel for your hens to lay eggs.

TIME TO BUY

It is advisable to buy birds from a reputable seller. Ideally, from someone who has been recommended to you. So, if you have a friend or neighbour who keeps chickens, don't be afraid to ask them where they bought their birds. This will cut down on the likelihood of buying unhealthy birds. A poultry seller with a good reputation won't sell you a cockerel when you want a hen, or an old bird that has stopped laying. If you are in any way like I was when I started out, then, let's face it, you are unlikely to know the difference.

If you are introducing birds to an existing flock, always quarantine them for at least two weeks to ensure they are in good health before they mix with your existing flock. During this time you can observe, worm and delouse them as necessary.

EGGS, EGGS AND MORE EGGS!

Humans have used eggs as a source of food for millennia. They are an important and well-balanced source of essential nutrients such as zinc, iron and vitamins A, B12, D and E. You'll never go hungry if you have eggs. From the humble fried, poached or scrambled egg to frittatas and pavlovas, they are an incredibly versatile (and tasty) food. Imagine having the luxury of this food in your own back garden. They also provide a great excuse to make cakes and other baked goods.

STORING YOUR EGGS

I never keep my eggs in the fridge. They will remain fresh at room temperature for at least three weeks. If you're not sure whether your eggs are fresh or not, use the following simple method to check:

1. Fill a large bowl with water.
2. Gently put the egg into the water.
3. If it sinks it's fresh.
4. If it stands upright it is at least a few days old.
5. If it floats to the top the egg is bad and should not be used.

> It is much easier to peel an egg that is a couple of days old, so use your older eggs for hard-boiling.

Have you ever cracked an egg and seen either a brown or red spot in the albumen (the white of the egg)? It's not unusual to find either of these, but don't worry – they're both harmless if eaten. A red spot is most likely to be what's called a 'blood spot' and comes from a ruptured blood vessel. A brown spot or 'meat spot' is usually caused by a tiny piece of the reproductive system being caught in the production of an egg. If you like, you can remove them, but the egg is completely edible.

Egg Issues

Not every egg emerges as a perfectly formed work of art. There can be some glitches along the way. For example, when a hen lays her first egg, it might be very small (the size of a quail egg) or there may be some streaks of blood on the shell. If your hens are not getting enough calcium they may lay eggs with a very soft shell or no shell at all. As a hen gets older, she will start to lay less frequently, but the size of her eggs will increase. It is not unusual to find two yolks (or even three) in eggs laid by older hens. Small and soft-shell eggs can be discarded.

CHICKEN HUSBANDRY

Bedding

My first rule of good chicken husbandry is to ensure that your chickens always have clean bedding. Dirty bedding leads to a build-up of ammonia, which is likely to lead to a respiratory infection in your birds. This is easily preventable by changing the bedding regularly. A weekly clean-out should be sufficient, or more regularly if necessary. I find that medicated milled straw works very well because it is super absorbent. However, be it straw or shavings, the key to good husbandry is to keep the coop and bedding as clean and dry as possible.

FEEDING YOUR CHICKENS

Grit

You have probably heard the saying 'as rare as hen's teeth'. Well, that's because hens don't have any teeth. And neither do cockerels for that matter. They grind their food down in their gizzard (a muscular pouch similar to a stomach). The grinding process is aided by stones and grit that the hens pick up while they are foraging. They will get a certain amount of grit to help with digestion by free-ranging, but I always leave a container of grit out for them to ensure they have an adequate supply. This helps prevent conditions like impacted crop (see page 31). Grit is not expensive. I use oyster-shell grit, which contains calcium that helps the hens produce great egg shells.

Food

Following years of research, poultry feed companies have produced a pellet that includes all the nutrients a chicken needs. There are optimum levels of proteins and nutrients that a laying hen requires, and all this goodness can be found in a 'layers pellet' or 'layers mash'. Poultry pellets/mash can be bought at any farm and feed store, pet store or veterinary store. After that, the choice is yours: do you want to buy an Irish feed, the cheapest feed, a non-GM feed or an organic feed?

Some poultry keepers suggest that you don't need to use layers pellets and that your hens will lay on a diet of wheat and scraps. However, I take the view that for a small-scale poultry keeper the cost of a bag of layers pellets is relatively inexpensive and will last quite a while, so why not give them a feed that has all the nutrients they require?

Occasionally, I give my flock wheat as an afternoon treat. In winter, I give them oats (made up like a porridge) to keep them warm. I sometimes also give them scraps. Leftover potatoes and vegetables, pasta and rice are always well received. Again, this is just a treat, but one that the chickens love. Regardless of what else I give them, I always make sure they have pellets in the morning so I know they are getting all the nutrients they require.

Water

It's thirsty work laying eggs and your chickens may drink up to half a litre of water each per day. It's very important to keep your drinker clean and filled with fresh water. Adding apple cider vinegar once a month (see page 28) will also prevent a build-up of green algae in your drinker.

Poultry feeders and drinkers come in all shapes and sizes and to suit all budgets. They are readily available online and in pet and agricultural stores.

CHICKEN BATHS

Unless you are keeping show birds or your chickens get particularly dirty, there should be no real need to wash them. Chickens clean themselves by having dust baths and preening. Any area of dry soil can become a dust bath for your chickens and, believe me, they will find it for themselves. If your chickens do not have access to dry soil, you can create a dust bath in your run or under your coop by placing soil and sand in a shallow container – something like a big old roasting tin would work really well – and the chickens will do the rest. You could also sprinkle some louse powder in this soil to ensure that they rid themselves of any parasites they might be harbouring.

Here at Hunters Lodge I occasionally wash my white Silkies. They have more fluff than feathers, so if they get really dirty during the winter I give them a wash in spring.

To wash a chicken, place it in tepid

water and use a mild dog or baby shampoo. Create a lather and gently wash the feathers, ensuring no suds get in the bird's eyes. Towel-dry the chicken to remove excess water, and then, while holding the bird firmly, blow-dry its feathers on a low heat until dry. Keep the chicken somewhere warm overnight to ensure it is completely dry and to avoid it getting a chill.

HEALTH ISSUES

Now, don't panic, but I'm going to talk about lice, mites and worms. Chickens in general are very hardy, healthy creatures but, just like your cat or dog, they sometimes suffer from minor health problems. With some basic knowledge, you can ensure they have a great quality of life.

Worming

A build-up of worms can make your birds unhealthy and may cause them to stop laying, so a little preventative action is the way to go, particularly if your chickens are confined to a run. It's a good idea to worm your flock twice a year. Whether you use a medicated or herbal wormer is up to you, but both are easily available from veterinary and farm supply stores.

For one week every month, I add apple cider vinegar to my chickens' drinkers each day (20 mls of vinegar per litre of fresh drinking water). This helps make their guts inhospitable to parasites and gives them lovely shiny coats. This is an additional preventative measure and doesn't replace worming.

Lice and Mites

Check your chickens regularly for lice and mites by lifting their feathers so you can see their skin. I find that the best time to handle chickens is at dusk when they have returned to roost in the coop. This way, you can easily take a chicken out of the coop without stressing the bird by chasing it around the garden trying to catch it. The back of the neck, just up from the shoulder blades, and around the tail feathers are good areas to indicate whether your bird is infested.

Chickens that have access to dust baths are less likely to have

parasites, but it's still important to check them regularly. There are many products on the market which help protect your chickens from attracting parasites. Again, it's up to you to decide which product suits your needs (i.e. natural versus medicated). I choose natural products, but if you prefer something stronger there will be a medicated product to suit your needs. If you are introducing new birds to your flock, it is *very* important to treat the new birds for parasites while you have them in quarantine.

Red Mite

You won't find this mite on your birds but in the coop, particularly in the nest boxes and crevices. These little mites come out at night, crawl on the chickens and suck their blood. If you notice your chickens are reluctant to use the coop or nest boxes it may be a sign that you have a red mite problem. If you have a brand new coop and you are cleaning it regularly you are unlikely to have red mites, but older coops should be checked regularly. To keep red mites at bay sprinkle a little mite powder in the coop during your weekly cleanout.

Northern Fowl Mite

This mite lives on chickens and can have a detrimental effect on them. If present, the northern fowl mite will be visible on the bird's skin (particularly around the tail area), so regular checking and preventative treatment are a must. The tell-tale signs of a chicken with northern fowl mite are wet, greasy-looking feathers and signs of general lethargy. If you notice these signs, take action quickly, as these blood-sucking mites will very quickly make your bird anaemic.

Scaly Leg Mite

I find that this is more of a problem with the older birds in a flock. The scaly leg mite burrows under the scales of the legs, and you will know a bird has a problem when you see the scales becoming raised and encrusted. Over-the-counter treatments are available, but if the skin is not broken you can dip the affected legs in surgical spirits. Dip the chicken's legs into the liquid so that the legs are fully coated. This will prove to be immediately effective. In extreme cases you may have to repeat the process. These mites spread rapidly between birds and, as they cause intense irritation, any affected bird should be treated immediately.

Like I said, chickens by their very nature are healthy little creatures. They can withstand freezing temperatures and have the sense to get in out of the rain. With a little care and attention they will lead happy, healthy lives. Good husbandry is the key to keeping chickens successfully. Sometimes, however, even with the best will in the world, certain problems do still develop.

Respiratory Infections

This was not a big problem when I started keeping chickens, but in recent years it has become a huge issue. This is why it is so important to buy your birds from reputable sellers and quarantine any new chickens if you have an existing flock.

Symptoms of a respiratory infection include sneezing, wheezing and foamy eyes.

If you suspect your chickens have a respiratory infection, you will need to visit your vet and get an antibiotic for them. The most commonly used antibiotic for respiratory infections in chickens is Tylan. Your vet will instruct you on how to administer the antibiotic, egg withdrawal (if there is a period of time during which the eggs cannot be used for human consumption), and so on. You should isolate the sick bird immediately, but your vet will probably recommend that you treat the entire flock. Whenever this happens, I add garlic and some rosehip syrup or honey to all the water drinkers to give the chickens an added boost.

A build-up of ammonia in dirty bedding can lead to a respiratory infection, so be sure to keep your beds clean. I also suspect that wild birds may be the cause of some respiratory infections, but I've yet to prove it!

Impacted Crop

A chicken's crop (the first part of the digestive system, which stores food until it is passed into the gizzard) is located just beneath its neck. When the bird eats, the crop fills. As the food is digested the crop reduces in size. If you notice that a bird is off its food and its crop appears swollen throughout the day, it may have an impacted crop. This means that the food it has eaten has not passed into the gizzard and has become an impacted, hard lump in the crop. When this happens your chicken can no longer digest food, so it is important to clear the impaction as soon as possible.

If you suspect an impacted crop, take all solid food away from the chicken (but do not remove its water supply). Pour 2–4 mls of olive oil down the bird's neck very slowly so as not to stress the bird. The easiest way to do this is with a syringe, which is readily available in any pharmacy or veterinary store. Massage the crop gently to help break up the impaction. This may have to be repeated several times. If the impaction is bad, you may have to pour tepid water down the bird's neck, massage the crop, turn the bird upside down and try to release the water.

Only turn the bird upside down for a couple of seconds at a time. Leave the bird on a diet of natural yoghurt (this will help soften any remaining food and neutralise bacteria) and water for a couple of days until you are sure the impaction has cleared.

If there is no improvement after three days, contact your vet.

> To prevent impacted crops, always ensure your chickens have a plentiful supply of grit, and don't allow your birds to forage in long grass as this can often be the cause of the impaction.

MOULTING – OUT WITH THE OLD AND IN WITH THE NEW ... FEATHERS

When a chicken sheds its feathers and grows new ones, the process is called 'moulting'. This usually occurs once a year, typically in late summer/early autumn. In my experience, while cockerels and hens both moult, the hen's moult can be much more dramatic. Poultry keepers are also usually more aware of the hen's moult because they are likely to temporarily lose their egg supply. Hens may have 'light' moults when they are young, but moulting usually does not occur until after the first laying season.

If you are not familiar with this happening it can be quite alarming. The bird's feathers will start to fall out (beginning with the feathers on the head and gradually moving all the way down to the tail), and your hen will look completely bedraggled and may be quite subdued. The moulting process can take anything from six weeks to several months. During this time, egg production will be greatly reduced or may stop altogether. In my experience, the best layers tend to have the most extreme, but also the quickest, moult. Moulting and egg production are not mutually compatible because during a moult your hen will use all its protein to produce new feathers instead of eggs. This break in egg production gives the reproductive tract an opportunity to rejuvenate and may actually increase egg production when the hen returns to laying.

Just because a hen is not laying does not mean she won't

require layers pellets. The pellets will ensure that your hen receives all the nourishment she requires, which is particularly important during moulting. Extra protein such as sardines or mealworms will also be very well received at this time. Adding a clove of garlic to your chickens' water will boost their immune systems and stave off colds. Just remember that without feathers, your hens will really feel the cold, so be sure to provide them with plenty of shelter from the wind and rain.

WING CLIPPING

Wing clipping is the most common method of preventing chickens from flying. Clipping wings is a simple and painless process, but you must remember to clip only *one* wing on each bird. By doing this your chicken will be off balance and thus not able to fly. To clip a wing, spread it out and cut the bottom layer of feathers. Do not be tempted to cut the next layer of feathers as this is not necessary. While this may solve the problem of chickens flying up on boundary walls and into neighbouring properties, it also means that they can't fly away if a predator attacks, so it is very important to ensure that they are properly secured at night. After a chicken has moulted and its feathers have re-grown, you will need to clip one wing again.

HATCHING CHICKS

BROODY HENS

Some breeds of hens are known to make great mothers. They like nothing more than to sit on a clutch of eggs for three weeks and hatch out a brood of chicks. They may do this several times in the one season if allowed. Spring, when the days start getting longer and egg-laying is in full flow, is when you are most likely to find your hens becoming broody (also known as sitting, clocking or hatching). As the summer ends and the days start to get shorter again, hens are less likely to be broody. It's as if they know that hatching late in the summer means their chicks would be subjected to the harshness of winter – so they always wait until spring.

Breeds like Light Sussex, Orpingtons and Silkies are known for these broody characteristics. A good indicator that your hen is becoming broody is when she doesn't want to come off her nest in the mornings. She will definitely squawk and may even peck at you if you try to disturb her. On closer examination you will see that the feathers on her breast area are now gone; this

allows her direct contact with her eggs so she can keep them at the ideal temperature. Throughout the day she will turn each of the eggs several times. Some hens leave the nest during the day to go in search of food and drink, while others go into a trance and will not move for days. If your hen is not moving, it is very important that you lift her off the eggs once a day to ensure that she eats and drinks. It takes 21 days for chicks to hatch.

For those with broody hens, rearing chicks requires the smallest of input, as Mother Hen will do all the work. You will have to be much more hands-on with chicks hatched in an incubator.

INCUBATORS AND BROODERS

There are many types of incubators on the market – manual, semi-automatic and fully automatic. What type you choose will more than likely depend on the amount of free time and money you have available to spend. Whatever you choose, follow the manufacturer's guidelines closely to ensure that your incubator has the correct temperature and humidity settings. This will help you get the best hatch after 21 days.

After your chicks have hatched out in an incubator, you will need to move them to a brooder within 48 hours. A brooder is a secure area that will afford your chicks space but also keep them warm. Ensure the chicks are dry and have fluffed up before you move them so they don't catch a chill. Brooders are available to purchase, or they are very simple to make, with various designs available online at no cost. The heat source for your brooder can be an infra-red lamp or what is known as an 'electric hen'. This is a type of a hot plate for the chicks to stay under which replicates the warmth provided by their mother.

FROM CHICKS TO GROWERS

Once your chicks have reached the age of six weeks, they are called growers. If you have reared them in a brooder, it is at this stage that you will introduce them to your garden, which more than likely will already be home to other chickens. This step into the outside world may put your chicks at risk of getting Coccidiosis, a disease caused by a parasite found in the droppings of older birds. The parasite which causes Coccidiosis is not detrimental to a mature bird but can be lethal to a chick or grower. Symptoms include lethargy, 'huddling' (all the chicks will huddle together for warmth) and blood in their stools. You will see a very quick deterioration in the health of an infected bird but, if treated quickly, this can be cured. Treatment is available at your local farm/veterinary store.

Nowadays, most commercial foods contain a 'coccidiostat', an agent that acts as a preventative measure against Coccidiosis. I usually add apple cider vinegar to the chicks' drinkers (5 mls per litre) from their first week to help them build up their resistance to parasites.

If you are raising ducklings, do not use a feed that contains a coccidiostat as it is extremely detrimental to their health.

CHICKS: FEEDING AND DRINKING

For the first six weeks, I feed my chicks a specially formulated chick crumb. This contains all the nutrients they need and is widely available from farm and pet stores. It is perfectly fine to feed your chicks mashed, hard-boiled eggs for the first couple of days until you source some chick crumb.

After six weeks of age, when your chicks have moved on to the 'grower' stage, they will move from chick crumb to specially formulated growers pellets that are widely available in farm shops.

Chicks need to be provided with clean water to drink, but they may drown if their drinking container is too deep or if they find an open source of water. Miniature feeders and drinkers, specially designed for chicks, are available to purchase in most farm shops. If you don't have one of these, you can use a small, shallow container filled with water. A good tip is to put some large pebbles at the bottom of the drinking container to prevent drowning.

SO, WHERE DO I START?

I recommend that beginners start with a few point-of-lay birds. These are female birds aged between 18 and 25 weeks that are just about to lay their first egg. This is the simplest way to start and, as you gain more experience, you can add more hens, Mr Cockerel and maybe even consider hatching some chicks of your own.

If I had listened to people, I would never have bought my first hens, and I would have missed out on so much – a hobby for all the family, therapeutic time for me and, of course, the finest, freshest eggs. When I started poultry keeping, there weren't the tonnes of poultry books, the myriads of poultry forums and the popular poultry sales that we enjoy today. It was

me and my little book (totally unglamorous and not a photo to be had), but I muddled through. But you don't have to muddle through – this chapter has more than enough information to get you started. I have put the years of research in, now all you have to do is take that next step.

Ready, Steady, Sow!

3

*I*F YOU ARE NOT GROWING any food at the moment, where do you start? Your everyday commitments won't stop just because you have decided to take an active role in producing foodstuffs for the table. Your time is valuable, and for most of us it's in short supply a lot of the time. In Chapter 1, I spoke about taking your growing journey one step at a time, and that really is the best way to get started. Think 'easy to grow' and 'low maintenance' and you will get your self-sufficiency journey off to a very successful start.

I cover popular vegetable varieties in the next chapter, but I recommend herbs, tomatoes and salads to begin with. They are easy to grow and a great way to start. You don't even need to step outside your door to grow a lot of this food successfully. I presume you have windowsills? So, if the fact that you don't have a garden or a greenhouse has been holding you back, fear not – very soon you will be crossing tomatoes, parsley, chives and salads off your weekly grocery shopping list.

QUALITY TIME

If you have children, there's no better way to show them first-hand where their food comes from than by sowing seeds. In my opinion, this is a truly super way to spend quality time with your children. What child doesn't like to bury their hands in soil? We are fortunate to have a superb garden centre near us at Hunters Lodge, and when the children were younger we spent lots of quality time together there. Spending their few euros on a packet of seeds was serious business indeed! The packets were examined closely for details like how many seeds they would get for their money. A playground at the back of the garden centre and a coffee shop where we planned how the children would spend their pocket money was all we needed for a perfect outing. Such simple fun. I must also confess that the cakes in the coffee shop were – and still are – a huge attraction for me!

My grandparents would no doubt be horrified at the cost of seeds today, or even the amount of unnecessary gadgets available nowadays, but this I know for sure: they would all be proud to know that their great-grandchildren do not – and never did – think that their food originates in a supermarket.

If you are reading this book, chances are you have a keen interest in good, basic food. I'm sure you, like me, find it incredulous that some children don't know where milk, eggs and vegetables come from. Imagine if those children got to sow some seeds.

READY – HOME-MADE PLANT SPRAYS AND FEEDS

When I'm sowing and growing, I try to adhere to a chemical-free policy. Hunters Lodge is not a licensed organic garden, but that doesn't mean that I can't buy organic seeds and abide by all the principles of organic growing. I grow and rear organic produce for my family (sometimes selling any surplus at the gate) and take great comfort in the knowledge that the food my children eat has not been doused in chemicals. Composting and crop rotation are covered in the next chapter, but let's get started in this chapter with some basic home-made sprays and feeds. These are very economical and will come in handy, especially if you are growing herbs and tomatoes on your windowsills.

HOME-MADE APHID REPELLENT

Just because I try not to use chemicals and grow my food as organically as possible doesn't mean the local aphid population will respect my wishes and stay away. Ladybirds and hoverflies, being natural predators of aphids such as greenflies, help me enormously in the garden, but there are still times when the old greenfly takes up residence on my windowsills and I have to take action. Once an aphid takes hold, it punctures the plant and sucks out its sap. This immediately starts to weaken the plant, so the sooner action is taken the better.

To arm myself against aphids, I make up a simple garlic spray to have on hand throughout the growing season. This method requires the use of washing-up liquid. Using the spray without washing-up liquid is a good preventative measure, but it won't be effective enough if aphids have taken up residence on your plants.

> The following recipe is yet another reason to grow your own organic, intensely flavoured garlic.

Garlic Spray
Ingredients

- 2 cloves of garlic (press the garlic, don't chop it finely or it will get caught in the spray nozzle)
- Squirt of washing-up liquid
- ½ litre water
- 1 spray container

Method

1. Put all the ingredients in the container and shake well.
2. Spray as required

> Remember to also spray the underside of the plant leaves.

HOME-MADE PLANT FEED

Thanks to our chickens and pigs, there's no shortage of fertilizer here at Hunters Lodge. We have the finest compost on hand, and the soil in the vegetable garden is in great condition. But what if your soil is lacking in vital nutrients? Or you are growing in containers and your plants have limited access to the nutrients they require? My own fertilizer will work wonders in these situations, but I also make a nettle and comfrey tea, which is packed with nutrients and perfect for feeding hungry tomato plants. And the cost? Nothing!

You will find comfrey growing wild in hedgerows all over the country, usually beside streams and rivers. You can also grow it in your garden, but be careful as it will take over in no time at all. I like to forage for mine, and I have a particular place that I visit in late spring each year to collect my leaves. In my grandmothers' time, comfrey was used to help knit broken bones back together (it was also known as 'knitbone' because of this).

If you can't find comfrey, make a simple nettle tea. I've never known anyone to complain about a shortage of nettles in this country! Nettles love fertile soil and, if you don't have a supply in your own garden, woodlands, hedgerows and riverbanks are usually amass with them.

Comfrey and Nettle Tea
Method
1. Fill a 10-gallon plastic drum halfway with a 50–50 mix of comfrey and nettles (if you don't have both, you can make the tea with either comfrey or nettles).
2. Fill the drum to the top with water.
3. Seal the drum and leave it outdoors in a sheltered spot for 2–3 weeks.
4. When the smell is truly putrid, the tea is ready to use. The liquid will be very dark, and I dilute it until it becomes a nice golden colour before using. This gives me a top-class, organic feed for my tomatoes at no cost at all.

☺ STEADY – HARDENING OFF ☺

This book is all about the basics. It's about getting started. I'm not going to get you bogged down in fancy terms and never-ending explanations. But before we begin growing, I just want to explain 'hardening off', which will pop up almost any time we talk about seedlings, and then we're ready for the off.

If you are growing your seedlings indoors with the intention of planting out in the garden, it's important to harden off your young plants before you transfer them to the garden. To harden off your plants, bring them outdoors on a fine day for about an hour. The next day bring them out for two hours, and so on. Do this for about a week, by which time your plants will have become accustomed to outdoor conditions.

As seedlings start to grow, I like to run my hand very gently across the top of them to help strengthen them. I learned this trick from a tutor of mine years ago, and it really works.

🍎 SOW – BUY A PACKET OF SEEDS AND 🍎 GET GOING!

Herbs

I find it hard to believe that, once upon a time, I used to buy all my herbs in the supermarket. You know those little bunches of fresh herbs, definitely not organic, absolutely expensive, and always sealed in plastic packaging? When I think of it now I could cringe.

Of course, over the years I also occasionally bought a pot of parsley or basil to try to grow at home. Watching it wither away on the windowsill (usually from lack of water) was testament to the fact that I didn't have green fingers. Sound familiar? Every summer I hear the same story at my classes and demonstrations, usually featuring a poor old pot of parsley that died a quick death on a sun-baked windowsill.

You have to water your plants regularly if you want them to live. If you can commit to watering (or at least checking to see if they need water), then you're well on your way to growing success.

Does It Need Water?

If you stick your finger into the soil around the plant and it comes out bone dry, your plant needs water. The more soil that sticks to your finger, the wetter the soil is. You can also buy a little hydrometer to give you an indication of how much water your plant needs. They are not expensive and are a little more accurate than your finger.

In my experience, herbs will not do well in waterlogged soil. They like to be kept moist, but don't overdo it, and certainly don't leave them sitting in water. As a lot of herbs originate from sunnier climes, they benefit from sunshine, so they do really well on windowsills and in glasshouses.

When I first decided to grow herbs, I took myself off to the garden centre and bought pots of parsley, basil, chives, mint – the usual herbs. As they only cost a few euros each, it didn't seem expensive at all. And compared to supermarket prices, it wasn't. Back then I had no idea of how many seeds I could get in a packet for those same few euros. By sowing a packet of seeds, I not only have more than enough herbs for myself, but plenty of pots to give visitors, family and friends. Let me tell you, people love to receive a pot of the most divine-smelling organic parsley for their windowsill.

Types of Herbs

Herbs can be:

- 🌀 **Annual** – they complete their life cycle in one year, i.e. they yield their seeds at the end of the first year.
- 🌀 **Biennial** – they complete their life cycle in two years, i.e. towards the end of their second year they set seeds and die away.
- 🌀 **Perennial** – they have a life cycle of three years or more.

Examples of Common Herb Types

Annual	Biennial	Perennial
Basil	Parsley	Chives
Coriander		Oregano
Dill		Mint
		Rosemary
		Thyme

Sowing seeds works really well for annual and biennial herbs like parsley, basil and coriander. Perennials like chives are also easy to grow from seed. However, I would stick to buying plants when it comes to other perennials like oregano, mint and rosemary. When you are starting off, it really is far easier to start with pots of perennials.

Seed packets tell you everything you need to know before you get started, such as when to sow, when to thin out (seedlings may sprout too closely together and some might need to be removed) and the amount of watering required. It really is foolproof.

Nevertheless, don't buy too many packets to start with. Remember to start small and build up your selection as you gain some experience. One seed packet can contain a huge amount of seeds. In all likelihood you are not even going to need half a packet. You can seal and store the packet until next year, but chances are they might get lost or damp. What I tend to do is swap and share seeds with my friends. That way I usually have at least twice the varieties for half the cost.

The best time to buy your packets of seeds is in the spring. You will find them everywhere from garden centres to supermarkets. You can also buy them online from Irish suppliers. Resist the temptation to buy several varieties of the one herb. Trust me, you will have too many. Here's what to expect on the back of your seed packet:

- ⏱ **When to sow** – the recommended months to sow the seeds.
- ⏱ **Where** – this may be in trays of compost or individual pots.
- ⏱ **How** – specific requirements like watering, temperature and covering the tray.
- ⏱ **Care** – thinning out and potting on requirements.
- ⏱ **Harvest** – when you can expect to be using your herbs.

If you don't have your own compost, your local garden centre will have a range of composts to get you started. Seed trays are not expensive and you can sow your seeds or pot on (transplant your seedling to a bigger pot to allow it more space to grow and mature before you finally transplant it to the garden) the seedlings in recycled yoghurt pots or tins. Start asking your friends for old flowers pots that they might be throwing out (always wash thoroughly before use). If you are planning on growing herbs for gifts you can never have enough.

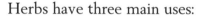

Always wash recycled pots thoroughly before use.

Uses of Herbs

Herbs have three main uses:

- ⏱ **Aromatic (culinary)** – herbs add colour, texture and immense flavour to dishes.
- ⏱ **Medicinal** – herbs have been used in healing remedies for thousands of years.
- ⏱ **Ornamental** – with its fragrant foliage and flowers, lavender is a perfect example of an ornamental herb.

Preserving Herbs

Air-drying works best for herbs like rosemary, thyme and oregano, as they don't have a high water content. I find freezing works best for herbs like mint and basil, as they contain a much higher water content.

Air-Drying Method

1. In late summer, while the plant is in its prime, cut healthy branches off your plant.
2. Wash the branches if necessary and be sure to allow them to dry fully. Wet herbs will go mouldy and rot.
3. Tie about six branches together and cover with a paper bag in which you have punched some holes. The bag will prevent dust settling on the herbs.
4. Hang the herbs in a warm room away from direct sunlight.
5. When they have dried out (this normally takes 10–12 days depending on humidity), store the herbs in an airtight jar.

Freezing Method

1. Pick the healthiest leaves during the plant's prime harvesting season (summer).
2. Wash if necessary and dry quickly.
3. Put parchment paper on a baking tray and place the leaves on the tray.
4. Put the tray in the freezer and remove when the leaves are frozen.
5. Now the leaves can be put into a freezer bag or container, and you can easily remove them a bunch at a time. Your herbs will last up to 12 months in the freezer.

The freezing process will make the leaves very limp when they defrost, but they will retain their flavour. This makes them ideal for use throughout the winter in soups and stews.

If you are starting out, try not to leave the garden centre with a dozen pots of herbs. If you can't maintain them, you will quickly lose interest in them all. Start with one or two basics (parsley and chives are popular and easy to maintain) and take it from there. Take it one step at a time and pretty soon you'll be wondering (just like me) how you ever bought herbs in the supermarket.

THE TASTIEST TOMATOES

I'm not quite sure how it started, but for many years now Eamonn has been growing tomatoes on our windowsills – delicious little cherry tomatoes packed with flavour that our children love to pick. In recent years he has also built a tomato house in the garden, and we've had our share of successes and disasters with it. Made from recycled glass doors, the tomato house is ideal for starting seedlings and growing salads, basil, tomatoes and cucumbers. In its early days it didn't have enough ventilation, and the plants succumbed to the high humidity behind its glass walls. We quickly sorted that out, however, and now we enjoy a plentiful supply of the tastiest tomatoes from our windowsills, the tomato house and the vegetable garden. The taste of these is incomparable to shop-bought tomatoes, and it's really worth giving tomato growing a go for the improved taste alone.

What to Choose

There are so many varieties of tomatoes out there – an incredible range of shapes, sizes and colours. If you are unsure about what variety of tomatoes to grow, I recommend that you start off with a cherry tomato plant. I find they usually produce more blossoms than the bigger fruiting plants so you have a better chance of them yielding fruit. Cherry tomato plants are also inclined to fruit earlier than larger varieties and are less prone to tomato blight as a result. You can grow tomatoes successfully in a pot on your windowsill, but bear in mind that the plant will grow quite high. A tumbling variety would be perfect for a hanging basket.

If you want a bigger or beefsteak tomato, there is a huge variety to choose from. I recommend starting with a Brandywine or Hillbilly plant. I grow tomatoes successfully from seeds but, if you prefer, you can get started by buying a plant. Buy the sturdiest plant you can find. If you find that the plant is stalky and willowy bury some of the stem along with the roots when you are planting it out. To do this, place the roots in the hole you have prepared as normal, but allow 2–3 inches of the stem above the roots to lie on the soil at the bottom of the hole. Cover this stem well when you are filling in the hole and securing the roots. This way the plant will grow more roots and anchor better in the ground.

Tips for Growing Great Tomatoes
Tomato plants like:

- **Full sun** – ideally eight hours of sunshine a day, so place them in a sunny spot.
- **Fertile soil** – as soon as the first trusses (bunches of yellow flowers – the flowers wither and are replaced by little green tomatoes) appear, feed the plant every week (see comfrey and nettle tea recipe on page 42).
- **Moisture** – water the soil, not the leaves, which will help stop the spread of any fungi.

If you are growing tomatoes from seed follow the instructions on the seed packet carefully. Like herbs, tomato seeds are normally sown in spring. You can expect to be picking the first of the cherry tomatoes by early summer. Keep in mind that the seeds will need strong sunlight to germinate (the sprouting of seedlings from seeds). Windowsills are perfect for this.

Upright and Bush Tomatoes

Tomato plants fall into one of two categories – upright (indeterminate) and bush (determinate). Upright, as the name suggests, means the plant will grow upright. It will need plenty of support as it grows (these plants easily reach to 6 feet and more). Bush means exactly that – it will grow like a bush (3–4 feet in height) and won't require the growing support that an upright tomato plant would. While an upright tomato plant will flower, produce and ripen fruit throughout a season, bush tomato plants tend to produce and ripen all of their fruit at the one time (usually within a week or two).

For upright tomato plant varieties, it's important to remove or 'pinch out' the side shoots between the main stem and the leaf stem. If they are allowed to grow, they will produce a mass of foliage and very few tomatoes.

Bush tomato plants don't produce an excess of side shoots, so they don't require the same pinching-out attention as upright plants.

When the tomato plant has produced seven or eight trusses, break off the growing tip of the plant. This will prevent the plant from producing more trusses and give the existing ones an excellent chance of producing top-quality fruit.

> Tomatoes like to be watered regularly. If you let your plants dry out and then flood them with water, the fruit will swell up and split. Regular watering will help prevent the fruit splitting.

LEAFY SALADS

In my grandmother Isabella's house, Sunday tea was often comprised of cold cuts of Sunday roast, fresh salad, freshly baked bread and a big pot of tea. Lettuce, tomatoes, hard-boiled eggs and slices of onion were all served up – good, basic foods, packed with flavour and nutrients. I can still taste it! Butterhead lettuce was freshly picked, washed and served in a great big bowl. My grandmother also loved to steam waxy new potatoes and serve them with a cold salad. Nowadays, I can pop out to my garden and gather the ingredients to recreate these wonderful memories. Yet, the salad leaves that adorn my table have come a long way from the humble butterhead lettuce. Not that there's anything wrong with butterhead; it is probably one of the most popular (and least expensive) types of lettuce bought in Irish supermarkets every week. However, if you want more variety, you will pay handsomely for it in a supermarket.

The mild climate of Ireland is perfect for growing lettuce.

Varieties of Lettuce

There are many varieties of lettuce available for you to sow and grow at home. Every year I buy what are known as 'cut-and-come-again' lettuce seeds. These are also called salad-bowl or loose-leaf lettuce leaves. Each of these seed packets contains a variety of lettuce types that can be cut as needed. After cutting the leaves off, they will grow again, hence the name. Each plant gives two or three yields throughout the season. Watch out for 'cut and come again' written on the front of the packet of seeds when you are buying them.

Having a supply of fresh salad leaves throughout the summer is a very achievable goal. If you are unsure about starting with seeds, your local garden centre will have a variety of young lettuce plants for you to choose from. Again, don't buy too many, as each one of these plants will mature at the same time, leaving you with a glut of lettuce which will likely be left unused. So buy a small amount to start with, and, three to four weeks later, buy a few more young plants. This way you will have a regular supply without any waste. These plants are ideally suited to outdoor planting.

If you choose to buy cut-and-come-again seeds, you can sow them in pots, in window boxes or in the ground. Sow thinly using about one-fifth of the seeds in the packet. After about three weeks or so, sow the next fifth of seeds, by which time the first fifth will be almost ready to harvest. You can start harvesting the plants when they have reached a height of 3–6 cm. Continue to plant throughout the spring and summer for a continuous supply.

If you buy a packet of lettuce seeds like iceberg or butterhead, you can sow them directly outdoors in late spring using the 'fifth' method described above.

Whether you choose to sow cut-and-come-again, butterhead or another variety, your lettuce will more than likely grow well, with minimal effort required.

For a continuous supply sow lettuce seeds a little at a time and sow them often.

You may enjoy some of the lettuces in your salad-leaf mix so much that you'll want to grow some individual heads of that variety. If that's the case, there are plenty to choose from. The following are some of my favourites:

Romaine

This is the lettuce leaf that you find in a Caesar salad. It is easy to grow, but be sure to thin seedlings, water well and pick leaves as soon as they are big enough.

Lollo Rosso

I love the rich, fiery, copper colour of these leaves. It will add a brilliant dash of colour to your greenhouse or garden. I use this as a cut-and-come-again lettuce by just picking the outer leaves. I find that Lollo Rosso is one variety that does particularly well in the sunshine.

Salad Rocket

This is definitely one of my personal favourites and is slightly less peppery than wild Rocket. It also has a faster growing time than wild Rocket: the leaves can be picked in 7–8 weeks.

Little Gem

Have you seen the price of this in supermarkets? Need I say more! Quick to mature at home in either a pot or a vegetable patch, Little Gem is very tolerant of hot weather and provides a deliciously sweet crunch to salad bowls.

Lamb's Lettuce

Also known as corn salad, this is a slow grower that I find great for winter harvesting. As temperatures drop, you may find you still have a supply of lettuce, but the taste may be somewhat sharper and definitely not as sweet. Not so with Lamb's Lettuce. Those slow-growing traits make it quite resistant to the drop in temperature that sees off so many of the other lettuce varieties. Lamb's Lettuce can be sown outdoors, but I sow it in the tomato house to have a supply of these deliciously nutty leaves throughout the winter.

ANYONE FOR RADISH?

If you like the peppery crunch of radishes in a salad, you're onto a winner when it comes to growing your own. These are very quick and easy to grow. You can sow directly into the ground but, because they don't require much depth, they are ideal for that container in the garden that's serving no purpose (you know the one).

Types and Growing

There are two types of radish: summer radish and winter radish. Winter radish is sown in July or August and harvested from October/November onwards, but summer radish is much more popular in Ireland. Radishes are extremely easy to grow from seed and, as I keep saying, everything you need to know will be on the packet. Nevertheless, here are a few little tips to help get you started:

- Like salad leaves, sow radishes in the spring and harvest them throughout the summer season.
- Sow every two weeks for a continuous supply.
- Radishes are ready to pick 4–6 weeks after sowing.
- Pick while tender and plump.
- Water regularly.

A Little Pot of Hot – Chilli Peppers

The chilli pepper is another little beauty that is easy to grow and will save you some money. If you like your food hot, it is a must. I recommend that you start with one established, healthy plant from your local garden centre. This should give you a plentiful supply of chillies. Some plants will continue giving you chillies right through to December if the conditions are right (a greenhouse is perfect or you can simply bring your plants indoors when the temperature starts to drop). I air-dry or freeze any surplus chillies and use them in stir-fries to add some welcome heat in the cold and dark winter months. If you have time and space, by all means buy a packet of seeds and follow the instructions carefully. I sow my seeds in March each year.

If you intend to grow chillies, keep in mind the following:

- Chilli pepper plants do not like the cold. I don't just mean mature plants. When you sow the seeds, keep your seed tray in a warm place. Make sure the plants don't endure a sharp drop in temperature at night.
- Once your seedlings appear, they need lots of light.
- Use your garlic spray if you have a green- or whitefly problem.
- Windowsills are ideal for chilli plants.
- I keep my chilli plants on a table in the tomato house and bring them indoors when the evenings get cooler.
- Don't over-water your chillies, but don't forget to water them either. Sticking your finger into the soil is a sure-fire way to know whether your plant needs more water. If the soil is not sticking to your finger give the plant a drink.

Chilli Pepper Varieties

There is a huge variety of chilli plants available: Cayenne, Jalepeno, Poblano and Anaheim, to name but a few. Have fun with peppers. When you realise how easy they are to grow, you'll be amazed at the amount of shapes, colours, sizes and heat levels that are out there.

> When cooking with your peppers, don't forget that the heat is in the seeds. If you want a milder taste, de-seed the pepper before using. If you decide to taste-test your peppers, have a glass of milk or some yoghurt beside you before you go chomping.

THE COOLEST CUCUMBERS

Starting off I was reluctant to grow cucumbers simply because I kept thinking we'd never eat a whole one. I didn't want to grow massive cucumbers only to watch them wither away in the fridge. Following my own 'one-step-at-a-time' principles, I wasn't thinking about making chutneys and pickles with them. I just wanted fresh cucumber to add to a salad, but without any waste. The solution? Mini-cucumbers! Perfection comes in all sizes, folks, and these were exactly what I wanted. When I started out, if I had too many of these cucumbers I gave them to friends and neighbours to enjoy. Nowadays, I still grow mini cucumbers, but I also grow the bigger ones. This allows me to make plenty of jars of cucumber pickle to accompany cold meats and home-made burgers for months on end. See page 120 for my cucumber pickle recipe.

Cucumber Varieties

The variety of cucumbers available is huge. Big, small, indoors, outdoors, crunchy, soft – the only difficulty you will have is limiting yourself to one or two seed packets. And, as the plants can grow up to 6 feet tall, it is important to consider the space you have available. I grow cucumbers successfully both indoors and outdoors. Passandra is an ideal indoor variety that will work well in a greenhouse or polytunnel. It gives me great yields in my tomato house. Many cucumber varieties grow well outdoors, with Marketmore being a popular choice for Irish gardeners. Mini varieties like Miniature White work well both indoors and outdoors.

Your cucumber seed packet is likely to contain between five and fifteen seeds. Place each seed in an individual pot and follow the packet instructions, which will include details on watering, potting on and transplanting (potting out).

Growing Tips

Cucumbers enjoy warmth, so they do particularly well in greenhouses and polytunnels. As the plants can grow up to 6 feet tall, I grow mine against a trellis in the tomato house. Cucumbers don't like to have their roots disturbed *ever*, so I start the cucumbers by sowing the seeds in biodegradable pots and then transfer the pot into the ground when the seedling is strong. Be careful if you are weeding that you don't disturb the root system. If this all sounds like too much work, you can buy sturdy cucumber plants in garden centres. Be gentle with the roots when you are transplanting them. And remember, *water, water, water*! As cucumbers are made up mainly of water, it is important that you give them plenty.

A FINAL WORD

If you want to kick-start all of the above by buying plants instead of sowing seeds, by all means do this. This really is about whatever you are most comfortable doing. It might cost you a little more for the plants, but in the long run it may be the route you need to take to save you lots of money down the line. And that's fine.

Speaking of saving money, you won't have much money left if you decide to go out and buy lovely new shiny pots and containers for your herbs and salads. Trust me, these are best left for the occasional splash. In the meantime, remember that even an empty tin of beans, cleaned out and with holes punched in the bottom, will make a perfect receptacle for herbs. Start thinking outside the box (or tin) when it comes to planting. There are lots of money- and space-saving ideas out there.

Here at Hunters Lodge, for example, we have a 'welly wall'. We punch holes in the bottoms of our old wellies, fill them with herbs and attach them to a wall. Space-saving and cost-effective! Music to my ears.

The Low-Down on Vegetables

4

AS A YOUNG GIRL, I did not live on a farm, but my dad always had a vegetable patch in the garden. Neat drills, impeccably maintained, provided our family with an array of nutritious produce. My particular favourites were the new potatoes and swedes – those swedes were to die for! I don't recall any of our neighbours having vegetables patches in their gardens but, of course, being only children, we took it for granted. We thought nothing of going out to the garden and picking some lettuce and scallions for sandwiches. It is only now I realise how fortunate we were and, who knows, maybe that's why we were always so healthy growing up.

My dad learned how to grow vegetables from his father, and I feel honoured to keep the tradition alive. It has definitely taken me a while, but I've gotten the hang of it now, and it fills me with such joy to see my own children growing seeds and picking their own lettuce leaves. At least they will take for granted the fact that vegetables grow in their garden, just like I did.

Even though my parents have sold our old house and they have a smaller garden now, Dad continues to sow and grow, and I love nothing more than to swap stories with him about how our vegetables are coming along. We exchange pots of herbs, and I continue to envy the neatness of his work. Maybe when I, too, retire, I will finally master the skill of weeding. In the meantime, I shall hide behind the word 'organic' as the reason for those areas of wilderness in my garden!

In this chapter, I will touch on some of my favourite foods to grow. In truth, this is only a snapshot of what you could grow in your garden. For the advanced gardener, there is already an array of books available that provide detailed information on every

vegetable on the planet, but my aim here is to stick to the basics. And remember, one of my golden rules for beginners is:

> Only grow food that you like to eat.

Before I delve into our favourite vegetable here at Hunters Lodge, I want you to consider two principles of organic gardening – composting and crop rotation – and why I think they are a huge part of chemical-free gardening. I will cover only the basics of these, but this will give you enough knowledge to set you on the right path.

COMPOSTING

You will reap huge benefits by adding compost to your soil, so why not consider having your own compost bin in the garden? Micro-organisms in the compost break down organic matter into nutrients that are hugely beneficial to your plants. While that alone would be enough, there are other advantages. What an easy way to help our planet by composting instead of dumping. Why say no to the finest, free fertilizer? Compost bins come in all shapes and sizes – I'm sure you have seen the plastic bins that are sold everywhere nowadays. Or, if funds are low, it is very easy to make your own compost bin using recycled wood or pallets. The most important thing for me when I'm composting is to get the ratio of nitrogen to carbon correct. I follow the 4:1 rule of nitrogen- to carbon-based foods and waste materials, which ensures a good breakdown of all the materials in the bin.

Nitrogen-to-Carbon Ratio

Nitrogen (also called greens)	Carbons (also called browns)
Vegetable peelings	Newspaper
Fruit peelings	Hedge clippings
Grass clippings	Straw bedding
Nettles	Egg cartons
Tea bags/coffee grinds	Toilet roll inserts

Remember the 4:1 rule for composting. A compost bin will take up very little room in your garden but will provide great benefits to your soil and plants.

COMPOSTING TIPS

- Be sure to stir your bin every couple of weeks. This will help the compost break down faster.
- If your compost is very dry and not breaking down, you may have too much carbon material in the bin. I add nettles or comfrey tea if this happens.
- If your compost is getting slimy, your nitrogen ratio is too high. Add straw or cardboard to resolve this.
- Place your bin in an area that receives lots of sunlight.
- Do not add cooked foods, whole eggs or fish to your bin. The smell of these foods will only invite unwanted visitors to your compost heap.
- The composting process can take up to six months, so be patient. Cut up cardboard and raw vegetables into small pieces to make the breaking-down process easier.
- When your compost is ready, it should be non-smelly, dark and crumbly

Now, that doesn't sound too hard does it? It is so easy to enjoy the finest chemical-free compost at little or no cost. If you don't already have a compost bin, I hope you will consider getting one.

CROP ROTATION

If you have vegetable beds, no bed should see the same crop in successive seasons. By rotating your crops each year, you avoid draining valuable nutrients from the soil, reduce chemical use, minimise pests and diseases, and maximise yields. Now don't be put off by the idea of crop rotation, it really is quite easy. Overleaf is a simple method based on four vegetable beds to get you started. As you become more experienced, you can add or remove varieties of vegetables and the amount of vegetable beds you use each year.

Simple Crop Rotation Method

Year 1	Year 2
Bed 1: Potatoes, carrots and parsnips	Varieties grown in Bed 1 in Year 1 should be grown in Bed 2 in Year 2.
Bed 2: Broccoli, turnips, cauliflower and cabbage	Varieties grown in Bed 2 in Year 1 should be grown in Bed 3 in Year 2.
Bed 3: Peas and beans (all varieties)	Varieties grown in Bed 3 in Year 1 should be grown in Bed 4 in Year 2.
Bed 4: Salad crops	Varieties grown in Bed 4 in Year 1 should be grown in Bed 1 in Year 2.

YEAR 1

YEAR 2

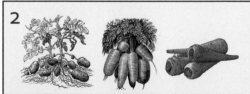

By using this method, plants that are heavy feeders and require a lot of nutrients follow those that are light feeders, and vice versa. For example, peas, which are fantastic for producing nitrogen in the soil, are followed by the likes of cabbage, which requires lots of nitrogen. Crop rotation is an ideal way to grow vegetables organically.

Here is my top tip for crop rotation:

> Keep a gardening diary.

A simple little copybook will do just fine, or you can use the notepaper at the end of this book. Write down the year and draw a rough plan of your vegetable plot. Mark each bed with the vegetable growing in it. When it comes to spring of the following year, your diary will be extremely useful in helping you to rotate your crops. Please don't think you are going to remember what crop was growing where because, trust me, you won't.

> 'Poached egg' plants will make a lovely addition to your garden. Scatter a packet of their seeds in a sunny spot and watch them grow. These little beauties will attract all the right insects into your garden and help you steer clear of pest-control treatments. Their lovely blanket of foliage topped with delightful yellow and white flowers provide a welcome splash of colour. Just be careful not to let them take over your garden!

☺ SENSATIONAL SPUDS ☽

I'm pretty much as Irish as you can get, and I can't think of a better way to start a discussion on vegetable growing than with a national favourite – the noble spud!

Let me tell you that when I go out to the garden and dig potatoes for dinner, I feel like I am *the* most successful gardener–

cook in the world! Walking only a few metres from the kitchen and collecting potatoes for our evening meal never ceases to give me a huge thrill. Because I'm using the potatoes immediately, and not harvesting or storing them, there's something really special about the experience. Follow that with cutting into a fresh head of home-grown broccoli, and I really don't think it's possible to get fresher or more nutritious food anywhere in the world. For me, because of our historical association with potatoes in this country, they sometimes act as a poignant reminder of our forefathers and the struggles they endured during the Famine. Of course, I don't think of this every time I'm digging potatoes in the garden but, occasionally, they serve as a reminder of how fortunate I am to have such sustaining produce at my fingertips.

What's more, growing potatoes is incredibly simple. I'm not going to confuse you with all the dos and don'ts – I'll give you my basic method, which works very well for me.

What You Will Need
- ☉ Seed potatoes (these look like small potatoes and are available in garden centres, usually in early spring)
- ☉ Coal sack/potato bag (if you don't want to dig a bed)
- ☉ Compost
- ☉ Time to water them, if necessary

You can get certified disease-free seed potatoes from a garden centre. It is possible to sow potatoes which you bought in the supermarket, but I like to ensure that my seeds are certified as disease free, and I recommend that you do too.

WHICH POTATOES TO CHOOSE

I divide my potatoes into three groups:

- First earlies
- Second earlies
- Maincrop

First Earlies

As the name suggests, these are the potatoes that mature first. They can be ready to harvest in as little as three months. Each year, I grow my first earlies in coal sacks in the garden. These are the potatoes that I use for salads and barbeques throughout the summer. They don't store well, so dig and use them as you need them throughout the summer months.

I prefer waxy first earlies, but there is a huge amount to choose from. Some of the most popular first early varieties are:

- Pentland Javelin – this variety provides one of the first waxy potatoes of the year.
- Duke of York – this is another popular waxy salad potato, and a favourite at Hunters Lodge.
- Home Guard – these make a perfect 'new potato'.

Second Earlies

Second earlies take two to three weeks longer than first earlies to mature. Again, I grow these in coal sacks in the garden. Like first earlies, these potatoes don't store well, so dig and use them as you need them.

Popular varieties include:

- Charlotte – this has long been a popular choice with Irish gardeners.
- Orla – the blight-resistant qualities of Orla make it a sure-fire hit every year.

🥔 Maris Peer – this is a reliable cropper of waxy potatoes.

Maincrop

These potatoes take up to five months to mature, and they store very well. Here at Hunters Lodge we grow these in drills in the vegetable garden.

Some of my favourite varieties include:

🥔 Rooster – one of the most popular varieties in Ireland, the Rooster is a great all-rounder.

🥔 King Edward (or 'King Eamonns' as we call them) – this variety is my personal favourite and one of the easiest to grow, yielding a huge crop of large, floury potatoes.

🥔 Sarpo Mira – this is one of the most disease-resistant potato varieties, which makes it perfect for the organic gardener.

CHITTING

Chitting potatoes is a process by which you encourage your seed potatoes to grow shoots. Growing shoots ahead of planting will give the potato a head start when it goes into the soil. This should give you an earlier harvest. I only chit my first and second earlies. It's a very simple process.

Four to six weeks before you plan to sow your seed potatoes outdoors, place the potatoes in an egg carton (or something similar) in an area with lots of sunlight. Place the potatoes so that

the side with the most dimples (or 'eyes') is facing up. It's important that the potatoes are not in an area where the temperature is likely to go below freezing. Light and warmth are the key to chitting. I use my windowsills and even my dining-room table for this job. Over the weeks, little shoots will appear on the potatoes. You are aiming for two or three shoots, each about 1 inch long. These shoots should be a purple–green colour. If your shoots are long and white, your potatoes are not getting enough sunlight. You only need two or three shoots on each potato, so rub off any excess. This ensures you don't have too many shoots sharing the nutrients in the soil, and it will also give you bigger potatoes.

Chitting is as simple as 1, 2, 3:

1. Buy the potatoes.
2. Put them on a tray in sunlight.
3. Wait four to six weeks.

THE NITTY GRITTY

So, you have a potato bag and compost, and your first earlies have chitted. Now all you have to do is plant them. Begin by rolling down the sides of the potato bag till it is about 12 inches in height. Put about 4 inches of compost in the bottom of the bag. Place three or four seed potatoes on top of the compost and cover them with a deep layer of compost (approximately 3–4 inches). That's it!

Each time green shoots appear, cover them with compost until you can no longer see them. As you do this, unroll the bag as the compost level gets higher. Continue covering the new shoots as they appear until you have almost reached the top of the bag. At this point, let the plants grow without covering new growth. When the plant flowers, wait for three to four weeks, and then your potatoes are ready to dig.

I grow my maincrop potatoes in drills, spacing the potatoes 12 inches apart and sowing them 4 inches below ground. As the shoots appear in the drills, I cover them with soil. Because potatoes usually grow towards the surface of the soil, covering them with fresh soil as they grow will help keep the sunlight out and prevent them from going green. It can also give the tubers some protection from blight.

Don't forget to water your potatoes. If we are experiencing our usual rainy weather there should be no need to water them, but if we have a dry day or two, give them a little water.

POTATO BLIGHT

There is one downside to growing potatoes in Ireland – blight. Some years it hits and that's it, almost overnight your crop is destroyed. You'll know the fungus has taken hold if you see little brown spots on the leaves of the plant. Sometimes you can save the tubers by cutting away and destroying all the infected vegetation.

One particularly bad year, I was lamenting to a friend about the loss of my crop. He suggested it was because I hadn't used chemical sprays. However, within a week, his chemically treated potatoes had succumbed to blight too. So, what can you do? Well, this is why first earlies are great, because they are usually harvested before the blight season kicks in. These days, I mostly grow blight-resistant varieties like Sarpo Mira and Orla. This gives me the best chance against blight. Potato blight is a nuisance when it occurs, but it's certainly not going to put me off sowing spuds every year.

Before I move on to talk about some of the other garden staples we grow here at Hunters Lodge, let me just remind you of what I suggested in Chapter 1:

> One step at a time – start small and build.

A GARDEN WITHOUT GARLIC?

I can't imagine our garden without garlic. It is easy to grow and thrives in freezing temperatures. It has been years and years since I have bought garlic in a shop. I know it's not the most expensive of items to buy, but why buy it at all when you can have your own supply of the most flavoursome garlic at your fingertips? This is a great starter vegetable too because if you don't have room in the garden for a vegetable bed, you can sow it in your garden border or even in pots. You definitely have no excuses for not growing garlic – unless of course you don't like it.

SOWING AND GROWING

You should buy the garlic bulbs you are going to sow from a garden centre. These are usually sold in packs of three bulbs –

enough to keep an average family in garlic. If you are serious users of garlic, buy a second packet – it won't go to waste. Break the bulb into cloves and plant them in the ground, spacing them about 6 inches apart. Sow in late autumn and the garlic will overwinter successfully. For a continuous supply, I sow more garlic in early spring. It is important not to allow weeds to build up in the bed. Because of its pungent odour, I find that garlic is resistant to most pests. When the leaves have turned yellow, your garlic is ready to harvest. This usually happens in July or August.

At this point, dig out the bulbs and leave them to dry, ideally in the sunshine. In the absence of sunshine (this is Ireland!), Eamonn hangs the garlic bulbs in the garage and leaves them to dry for a few weeks.

I'd love to tell you that we make fantastic plaits of garlic to adorn our kitchen but, alas, we don't do anything that glamorous. When the garlic is dry, I pull off the long leaves and put the garlic in a basket in my kitchen. There it stays perfectly fresh for months. You may find that home-grown garlic is quite strong so you won't use as much as with store-bought garlic.

By planting garlic twice a year, once in the autumn and again in the spring, I have a year-round supply. Not only do I use it for cooking, I also put garlic cloves in the chickens' drinkers occasionally to give them a home-made immune-system boost. Garlic makes a nice gift for visitors too.

ONIONS AND SHALLOTS

As with garlic, you may think that onions are so plentiful and inexpensive that it's not worth the effort of growing your own. That's fair enough, and if I had to choose between onions and shallots because space was an issue, I'd choose shallots every time. This is simply because shallots are inexpensive and easy to grow but are a costly item if I have to buy them in the supermarket. However, if you have a spare vegetable bed, you really can't beat the taste of a home-grown onion.

SOWING AND GROWING

Neither onions nor shallots are suitable for container growing. You can sow onions from seed, but I would recommend that beginners start off with 'sets'. A 'set' is a pack of baby/immature bulbs. Sometimes the onion bulbs are sold loose in garden centres. This is ideal, as you can pick your own bulbs. Choose a firm, medium-sized bulb. Sow the bulbs in March/April. Place the wide end of the bulb into firm soil with the tip of the bulb just above soil level. Sow the bulbs at least 4 inches apart. The wider the spacing, the bigger the onion.

You sow a shallot bulb just like an onion bulb. However, as the shallot grows, it forms a clump of about eight mature shallots.

When the leaves die away, onions and shallots are ready for harvesting. They must be dried out completely before storage.

PEAS

Peas are one of our favourite snacking foods in the garden every year. However, I have long ago given up on my grand plans of freezing enough of them to have a supply throughout the winter.

Instead, I encourage one and all to eat them fresh from the pods during the summer months. Their sweet flavour is absolutely and totally addictive, and they are bursting with goodness. If some of our peas do manage to make it to the freezer, I use them to make pea soup (see the recipe on page 122). But I don't worry about freezing too many. I'm happy to buy good quality peas in the supermarket if I don't have my own supply. They are not expensive and, because they are picked and frozen quickly, they still contain lots of nutrients.

If you remember eating peas from pods as a child, now is the time to recreate that memory. They are easy to grow from seeds and are ideal for starting on your windowsills in early spring. Be careful when hardening off (see Chapter 3) young plants if you have chickens. Yes, this is experience talking; I've lost many a pea shoot left on the patio for an hour to my nosey chickens.

The following are some important points to bear in mind:

- Peas like full sunshine.
- They need support – I use 6-foot canes to support mine.
- I sow my seeds indoors in early spring and transplant them into the ground in late spring when they have been hardened off and are sturdy.
- As the seedlings shoot up from the ground, keep the area between each plant weeded.

🫛 Keep picking your peas if you want your crop to continue. As you pick, the plant produces more flowers and pods.

🫛 Pick your peas from the bottom of the plant upwards, as this is usually where you will find the most mature pods.

🫛 Don't forget to water during dry spells.

🫛 Finally, why not consider adding a mangetout variety along with your regular peas? Mangetout have a soft skin and smaller peas, so there's no need for shelling the peas – eat the skin and all.

😃 ENDLESS POSSIBILITIES 🍐

Aren't we just flying along? Herbs, tomatoes, garlic, potatoes, peas – you'll never look at a windowsill the same way again!

OLDIES BUT GOODIES

Now start thinking about other vegetables that you like to eat. Remember I mentioned my dad's swedes earlier? Well, they are a must for me. My mother also makes a mean carrot-and-parsnip mash, and those two vegetables also make the list at Hunters Lodge. Oldies but goodies, I like to call them. If you are nervous about growing carrots for the first time, start with baby carrots and take it from there. These are quick and easy to grow from seed.

HEALTHY OPTIONS

I could eat broccoli till the cows came home, so I make sure to plant some every year. I know I should really refer to it as 'calabrese' ('broccoli' being its purple sprouting cousin), but we grew up calling it broccoli and that is what I know it as. I don't mind what it's called, so long as I have it growing in the garden. This is one vegetable that I freeze every year.

Cauliflower and cabbage are not as popular as broccoli here, so I grow less of these, and any surplus goes straight to the freezer.

Beetroot is another favourite of mine, and if you're looking for something that's practically foolproof to grow, then this is it. Beetroot can be grown very successfully in containers (10 inches × 10 inches), but if you have some space outside it's worth allocating some for beetroot. It's this easy:

- 🐝 Sow seeds directly into the ground in late spring.
- 🐝 Thin out the seedlings well.
- 🐝 Water consistently.
- 🐝 Harvest when they are almost the size of a tennis ball (this usually takes between 90 and 100 days).

MIX IT UP!

I like to add a splash of colour to my vegetable garden, and not just with vegetables. When I start sowing seeds in the spring, I also sow a tray of sunflower seeds. These are particularly easy for children to grow. They are fast growing and hardy. When they flower in late summer, they add a fantastic dash of colour to the garden. As they die off, we harvest, dry and eat the seeds.

I also sow sweet pea with my peas, and the flowers and scent are amazing. Their colours look so pretty amongst the pea tendrils.

BEE KIND

Whether you have beehives or not, I think it's important to have bee-friendly flowers in the garden. The bees could really do with our help. So, why not enjoy some of your favourite flowers in your vegetable patch and give the bees a helping hand at the same time?

MEMORY LANE

I often think there's a sort of seasonal nostalgia about vegetables. Kale reminds me instantly of my grandmother Stella and her colcannon. Oh boy, she made the *best* colcannon ever! As a young child I understood that I could only have colcannon when kale was in the shops. Back then, even in Dublin, if it was not in season, you didn't have it. So each year I'd wait for my colcannon. As a grown woman, I still visited my grandmother for colcannon every November. Now, I grow my own kale, but I wouldn't dream of eating colcannon out of season – it just wouldn't be right, and I wouldn't do my memories justice if I didn't wait until Halloween every year.

However, for me, there's nothing more seasonally nostalgic than sprouts. Remember how they used to be cooked in the ham water? Their saltiness oozing into your very core? Probably not the healthiest way to cook them but I loved that salt hit. These days, I mostly steam them, but they do occasionally find their way into the water used to boil our own garden-reared ham. It's a bit like fried bread – so bad but oh so good. I do think sprouts are a love-them-or-hate-them vegetable. I would happily eat them salty, steamed, soaked in butter or even cold. If you like sprouts, you should grow some. You'll have such fun picking them on Christmas Day – a talking point for the neighbours for sure.

Whatever vegetables you choose to grow, don't forget to enjoy the process. Remember that not everything you grow will be a success every year, but the disappointment associated with one failure will be balanced by a bountiful success with another.

A Fruity Tale

5

HOW I LOVE PICKING FRUITS in the garden. I love eating them even more. A lot of fruits are easy to grow, and they truly are gifts that keep on giving. Of course, some years there are problems – a late frost can wreak havoc with blossoms and wipe out many fruits, but, let me assure you, a good year makes you very quickly forget about the bad times. Nothing beats the taste of soft fruits grown on your patio or in your garden. Strawberries and raspberries packed with flavour and real goodness are no trouble to grow.

Need another reason? Last summer I was in a supermarket and I discovered that 150 g of raspberries cost €3.50! I'm not talking about an exclusive deli but a regular, run-of-the-mill supermarket. Well, earlier on that particular day I had dropped eggs to my friend Michéle's house. She wasn't home, so I left the eggs on the porch. Like me, she grows her own fruit and vegetables. After leaving the eggs, I noticed she had an abundance of raspberries, and I helped myself to a little snack. Later, after the shock of seeing the prices in the supermarket, I sent Michéle a text confessing to eating approximately €7 worth of raspberries from her garden! But, seriously, who can afford to feed their family with the freshest of fruits at that price? Buy some plants to grow at home, and I assure you that in no time you'll be making strawberry jam for your toast and raspberry lollies for your children. And even if you do nothing but eat your fruit straight from the plants, bushes or trees you'll be enjoying food in its most exquisite form.

My family's relationship with apple and pear trees has been bittersweet. In the early days of life at Hunters Lodge, we completely neglected the fruit trees that already existed in our garden as we worked our way around the clock. By the time we decided to get back to basics, the trees were diseased, and we were advised to cut them down and start again. It broke Eamonn's heart to have to do it, but cut them down we did so we could start again. It will be some years before we have huge windfalls of apples, but we get enough from our young trees for snacking, apple tarts and other bits and bobs. Michéle has wonderfully mature apple trees, and I have also had to confess to robbing her orchard on several occasions! Thankfully, she is very generous, and in exchange for her delicious apples we share our garden-reared pork and bacon with her.

Without taking up too much space in your garden, it is possible to grow fruits for gooseberry tart or redcurrant sauce.

I don't grow blackberries in my garden, as I much prefer to forage for them in the autumn, but you could consider including some blackberry bushes in your own garden.

So, pick a few of your favourite fruits and get growing.

☺ SWEET STRAWBERRIES ☺

When I think of strawberries, I think of two things — Wimbledon and my Granny Stella. She wasn't a farmer, quite the opposite in fact. But every year, in her leafy suburban home in south County Dublin, we would wait with anticipation for Wimbledon to start before we enjoyed our first strawberries of the year. It was our own little tradition, and boy did I love it! A big bowl of strawberries and cream, watching tennis on the television in the good old days of Bjorn Borg and John McEnroe — a magical memory for me, indeed. It's funny, but when I look back on those times it seems the sun was always shining ….

Every year here at Hunters Lodge, we watch and wait patiently to see if the strawberries are flowering well, then we wait for the sun to ripen them. When we finally bite into that first delicious, luscious red berry, it is truly worth every minute of the wait.

In sunnier climes, it's much easier to have a supply of ripe, succulent strawberries and for most of the year too. I recall visiting the home of some friends in southern Turkey some years ago. They had put out bowls of fresh strawberries like we would put out crisps and peanuts. I have never tasted strawberries like them. Eamonn and I had to hold ourselves back from devouring the lot. They have so much sunshine that ripe strawberries are taken for granted. We, on the other hand, are not so blessed in the sunshine department – but I think that makes our strawberries all the more special.

Strawberries are easy to grow and, best of all, they don't need much space. You can grow them on a windowsill, in a tub on a patio or balcony, or in hanging baskets. If you have a greenhouse they'll do very well, and if you have lots of space indulge yourself with a raised bed full of different varieties.

Strawberries are economical too, as the runners from Year 1 (these are horizontal stems containing miniature new plants that grow out from the mother plant during the summer season) can become your new plants for Year 2.

PLANTING STRAWBERRIES

If I am planting strawberries outdoors, I like to get the bed ready in late summer/early autumn. This allows the plants to get well established before the winter sets in. Pick a nice sunny spot, but one that will not be too exposed to frost.

Strawberries do very well in raised beds. Being raised, the soil warms up quicker than if it were on the ground, so you can plant a little earlier. This in turn means an earlier harvest. There is also less risk of waterlogging in raised beds, making them ideal for strawberries.

If you are concerned about harsh winters, you can postpone planting out your strawberry plants until the spring. If there is still a risk of frost when the plants have flowered, cover them loosely with newspaper or fleece at night. It really is worth taking this precaution.

GETTING DOWN TO IT

You now know when and where to plant the strawberries, so here's the how:

- ☺ Prepare the bed by digging well, loosening the soil and removing large stones. Avoid using a bed that has just grown soft fruits, potatoes or tomatoes. This is to avoid the possibility of the strawberries contracting soft fruit diseases, some of which may also be present in tomatoes and potatoes.
- ☺ Remove weeds and their roots.
- ☺ Mix in some well-rotted manure/compost to enrich the soil.
- ☺ Plant your strawberry plants with the crown just above the soil, about 14 inches apart.
- ☺ Water well.
- ☺ Be vigilant about weeding when the spring arrives and flowers start to appear on the plants.

HARVEST TIME

In late May/early June, when you start to see fruit on your plants, it is time to put down a mulch (straw works well) so that the strawberries are not sitting directly on the soil. This will help to keep them clean.

As the fruits ripen, pick them regularly and remove any rotten fruit.

It will inevitably become 'you versus the birds' when those red jewels start to ripen. I throw a net over my plants at the beginning of summer to ensure that I get a decent share of the bounty. But it's not just the birds that love them – you will have to be on slug alert at all times.

> Tip: Dry the shells from your hard-boiled eggs in a warm oven (very low heat for 20 minutes). Crush the dried shells and scatter them around vulnerable plants. Slugs are not so inclined to cross the shells. It doesn't work all the time, but this simple measure has saved many a plant for me.

FREE PLANTS

By August, when harvesting is over, give the bed a tidy up. Remove the straw mulch, cut back the leaves and remove debris. You will have noticed during the growing season that each plant has sent out runners. These will be running horizontally from the main plant and have new miniature plants along the stem. Simply take some small flowerpots filled with soil and sit them on the ground. Place each part of the runner that has a plant into a pot and secure it with a peg if necessary. Roots will establish in the pot – and you now have a new plant!

> Strawberry plants are usually productive for three or four years, and they should then be replaced.

IRRESISTIBLE RASPBERRIES

When autumn rapidly descends and all else has gone quiet in the garden, some of my raspberry bushes spring into life and provide

me with oodles of succulent raspberries through September and October. Autumn-fruiting raspberries are truly something special. Autumn Bliss is a good variety for red raspberries, and I recommend Allgold for yellow raspberries.

Add a few summer-fruiting varieties such as Glen Moy and Valentina and you can enjoy these luscious fruits from July right through to the first frosts in October/November.

Home-made jam, ice cream, raspberry gin and fruit pastilles are some of the delightful treats you can enjoy with these easy-to-grow fruits.

Raspberries also freeze very well. Freeze them individually on a flat tray first, and then bag them together when they are fully frozen. This way you avoid a mushy mess when they defrost.

PLANTING RASPBERRIES

Raspberries like free-draining soil. If your ground is prone to waterlogging, consider planting your raspberries in a raised bed where the soil can drain more freely. Like strawberries, prepare your bed in the spring and dig in some well-rotted compost. Consider planting varieties that fruit at different times during the year to extend the fruiting period. Your local garden centre will stock several varieties, or if your friends or neighbours have healthy raspberry bushes you could also plant some of their cut-offs in the spring and save yourself some money.

Raspberries grow best in full sunlight, but they also do quite well in less sunny spots. Provide a support system for the raspberry canes when you plant them (bamboo canes that you find in any garden centre will be fine), as they can grow up to 8 feet tall. It is best to have the supports in place before the bush becomes too unruly. Allow approximately 2–3 feet of space between your raspberry plants and weed regularly between the canes.

Cut back or prune all summer-fruiting canes after all the fruit has been harvested (July/August). Only cut back canes that have borne fruit. You can easily identify these canes with their tired-looking leaves, so different to the lush green leafy canes that will bear next year's fruit. Prune all the old canes right down to the ground just after harvesting. Remove any dead canes you find.

Cut back all autumn-fruiting canes in February (right down to the ground also). By cutting back well, you are limiting the number of canes availing of the soil's nutrients and creating air circulation which will help prevent disease.

If you have a sunny spot in your garden, it's well worth considering a couple of raspberry plants. Even if they don't make it to the kitchen or freezer, your raspberries will provide you with succulent snacks when you are pottering around in your garden.

RELIABLE RHUBARB

Rhubarb may, strictly speaking, be a vegetable, but to me it belongs in this 'fruity' chapter. I associate it with jams and tarts and ice cream – all things fruity and delicious – and it is a natural fit in this

chapter amongst the strawberries, gooseberries and apples.

Granny Isabella had an area of her front garden surrounded by a neat box hedge. In this 4 m × 2 m area, she grew the finest rhubarb in all the land. At least that's what we thought when we were growing up. She shared it with one and all and was probably responsible for half the rhubarb tarts in County Offaly during her lifetime. This is definitely how I picked up the habit of bestowing bunches of rhubarb upon every visitor to our home. I'm still taken aback when I see the price of a (quite often limp) bunch of rhubarb in the supermarket. The good news is it costs very little to have your own supply of fresh, chemical-free rhubarb.

Fresh rhubarb is the stuff of dreams. Rhubarb and custard, rhubarb tart, rhubarb jam, rhubarb compote – I can't imagine a garden without rhubarb. Unless, of course, you don't like it. Even if rhubarb isn't your thing, its big leaves are very attractive, and it can look quite nice in a flower bed. You can always give the stalks to your visitors throughout the season.

> Rhubarb rarely suffers from diseases, making it an ideal starter project.

Growing Rhubarb

If you would like to give growing rhubarb a go, here's how:

- Buy two or three rhubarb 'crowns' in your local garden centre or country market. This is plenty for the average family.
- Plant the crowns 2–3 feet apart in fertile, well-drained soil. I have planted crowns both in early winter and mid-spring successfully. Rhubarb not only tolerates but also requires a certain amount of frost, so don't worry if the temperatures dip really low after you have planted the crowns.
- It is advisable not to pull any stalks of rhubarb in the first year after planting, so the sooner you get it in the ground the sooner you'll have your own harvest.
- Rhubarb does grow and spread, so split your plants every four to five years. It's not difficult – in the winter when the plant is dormant, dig it up. Using a spade, divide the plant into three or four plants (crowns). Ensure that each crown has a 'bud'. This bud will provide next year's growth. Plant each new crown, covering the roots and bud completely (the bud should be approximately 1 inch under the surface). Now mark the spot with a stone or stick so you know where your plants are. As winter disappears and spring makes its welcome arrival, your rhubarb will also make a welcome appearance.
- In winter, when the leaves have died right back, cover the plant in manure. This will give the roots a nutrient boost and protect them from the elements throughout the winter.
- Rhubarb is very easy to maintain and requires very little work on your part. It enjoys sunlight and a good watering during dry periods.

> The leaves of a rhubarb plant should never be eaten, as they contain oxalic acid and are poisonous.

FORCING RHUBARB

This term simply means forcing your rhubarb to grow earlier than normal. The process is very easy. In late November cover your rhubarb crowns with a bucket or a bin (something dark that blocks out light). By January, your rhubarb should have started to grow, giving you a harvest when there is little else available in the garden. This forced rhubarb is perfect for wine-making too.

HARVESTING

When you are picking your rhubarb, choose the largest stalks first. Do not cut the stalks. Hold the base of the stalk, twist slightly and pull – the stalk will easily come away from the plant.

> A rhubarb crown should set you back no more than a few euros. A good investment indeed!

GLORIOUS GOOSEBERRIES

This is a prickly bush, let me tell you, but don't let that deter you. One bush can yield pounds and pounds of gooseberries, so invest in some good gardening gloves and away you go. A gooseberry bush will also grow well in a container, so if you are short on space consider growing gooseberries in a tub. Whether it's in the ground or in a container, I highly recommend having a gooseberry bush in your garden.

GROWING GOOSEBERRIES

Here are my top tips for growing gooseberries:

- Choose a sunny site for your gooseberry bushes.
- Plant your gooseberry bush out in autumn.
- If you are planting more than one bush, space them about 4–5 feet apart.

- Prepare the soil by digging over (dig and loosen the soil while removing large stones), removing weeds and adding some well-rotted manure.
- If you are buying bare-root bushes, dig a hole big enough so that you can spread out the roots.
- If you are buying your bushes in containers, dig a hole as deep as the container to plant out the bush.
- Water well until the bushes are established.
- During fruiting season, you will be battling with the birds again, so throw a net over the bushes to keep some of the fruit for yourself.
- Start picking your gooseberries (pick about a quarter of the fruit on the bush) in May/June. These gooseberries may be small but they are ideal for cooking with and, by picking them, you allow the remaining fruit to get bigger and sweeter – perfect for your main harvest in late July.
- It is important to water your gooseberry bushes well when they are fruiting.
- I prune my gooseberry bushes right back in winter. They need to be pruned really well to allow good ventilation when they start to grow again. Good air circulation is an easy preventative measure against both mildew and sawfly.
- Gooseberry bushes can be prone to mildew, but choosing a mildew-resistant variety should guard against this.
- Be on the alert for sawfly caterpillars. The sawfly usually lays eggs at the bottom of the bush and, as the caterpillars emerge, they munch on the leaves and travel upwards through the bush. Inspect the bush regularly (especially the underside of leaves) and remove any caterpillars as they appear. I've never had a problem with these caterpillars, but I'm forever vigilant.

RUBY REDCURRANTS

I think these are the prettiest little fruits to have in the garden. They look so elegant and delicate but, on more than one occasion, the birds have beaten me to them. Still, once I have enough for some redcurrant sauce, I'm happy. It's the perfect home-made accompaniment to venison, lamb, duck, and – my personal favourite – baked camembert. Home-made redcurrant ice cream is also sublime, but do remember to sieve the seeds out before using.

Growing Redcurrants

This is another fruit that's easy to grow and, if you have room, you could try a white or blackcurrant bush too. Planting currant bushes is similar to planting gooseberry bushes – they like a sunny site, fertile soil and should be planted at least 4 feet apart. Just remember:

- It is important to water your redcurrants, but over-watering during fruiting may cause the fruit to split.
- My plants don't have any trouble with diseases, but redcurrant plants can be prone to the dreaded sawfly caterpillar (see the section on gooseberries above), so do take action if you notice any signs of caterpillars.

TIME TO GET STARTED

So, there you have some of the basics – strawberries, raspberries, rhubarb, gooseberries and redcurrants. My advice to help you get started is to first identify a spot in your garden that would make a nice home for some fruit bushes. Go to your local garden centre and buy a fruit bush, and then plant it in that spot in your garden. While you are at the garden centre, talk to the staff. Ask them if there is a variety they would recommend. Don't be afraid to ask them for advice on growing. Remember, they work in a garden centre, and it's highly likely that they are well-trained and have a huge love of plants. I usually find that garden-centre staff are more than willing to impart their knowledge.

If you have only €5 to spare that's enough to get started. Remember my story about 150 g of raspberries costing €3.50!

🍎 AMAZING APPLES 🍐

After cutting down all our mature apple trees, Eamonn and I formulated a new plan. We chose an area of the garden and agreed that four new trees would be a good starting point (a tree for each of our children). We have since added a few more, but the four varieties we started with were as follows:

🍎 **Discovery** – Some years back my daughter Ellie and I watched a UK gardening programme. In it, the presenter was eating juicy red apples from her one-and-only apple tree in her small urban garden, a 'Discovery' variety. On the day Eamonn and I went off to buy our four trees, Ellie's parting words were 'don't forget to bring back a Discovery', and we did. This apple tree fruits early and, as it's not a fast-growing tree, it is quite suitable for smaller gardens.

🕐 **Katy** – Another good reliable cropper, Katy (or Katya), was chosen for our own daughter Kate. This is an easy-to-grow apple tree which produces deliciously juicy apples. The good news is that you can also buy a dwarf Katy in Irish garden centres now. Some trees are small enough to grow in patio pots.

🕐 **Bramley** – The cooking apple to beat all cooking apples! Traditional Bramley apple trees grow to a good size, but there are container-sized trees now available if space is an issue. Strong and reliable, this one was bought for our son, Joe.

🕐 **Ellison's Orange** – This was the fourth apple tree we chose. It is a mid-season fruiting tree and, while it is refreshingly juicy, it also has a hint of aniseed to it. It's an interesting one – just like our little Ruth!

Since then we have added some more apple trees – more Katy and Howgate Wonder, which is a good cider apple.

A spare fiver in your pocket is not going to get you an apple tree in your local garden centre, and miniature apple trees are slightly more expensive again. We paid in the region of €20 per tree for our four initial two-year-old trees. But then I got a little bit lucky: I discovered that a local fruit farm was selling off some of their apple trees. Three-year-old trees were being sold for €7 each – an amazing bargain! This allowed me to add to our orchard without breaking the bank. So, keep an eye out in the small ads in your area – you just never know.

When buying apple trees, or any fruit trees, be sure to get assurance that you are buying healthy trees. Also make sure you are clear on the pollinating requirements of your trees. The seller should be able to answer all your questions regarding the fruiting season, growing speed, pollination, and so on.

There are many varieties of apple trees to choose from, but here are some of the most popular in Ireland:

Common Apple Tree Varieties

Bramley	Elstar	Beauty of Bath
James Grieve	Katy	Golden Delicious
Jonagold	Gala	Discovery

> If there is a particular apple variety that you remember from your childhood, then that's the one for you.

Apple trees do well in most soils except waterlogged soil, so keep this in mind when choosing a location for your tree.
If space and money are an issue, put a dwarf apple tree on your birthday wish-list – you know you're worth it!

🍎 CRAB APPLES AND OTHER FRUIT TREES 🍎

If you are a fan of crab-apple jelly, you might consider growing a crab-apple tree. I have two crab-apple trees in my garden and, as well as the fabulous fruit, they produce a magnificent blossom in the summer. Of course, you could keep your garden space for something else and just forage for crab apples in the autumn.

Moving away from apples, you might consider plum or pear trees. Just remember the one-step-at-a-time rule. Fruit trees are more costly than soft fruit bushes, so it's important to think it through fully before you spend your money. Watch out for end-of-season deals in large DIY stores. I have lovely patio peach trees that I bought in the autumn at half price that are now producing delicious fruit during the summer.

🍎 ANYONE FOR ICE CREAM? 🍏

You can only imagine how popular home-made ice cream is here at Hunters Lodge. Picking fruit from the garden during the day for ice cream after dinner sounds idyllic, doesn't it? And you are wondering how on earth you would ever find the time to do this? Don't worry, I understand. I don't have hours to slave in the kitchen, and yet I always manage to have a stash of ice cream in the freezer. Some of our favourite ice cream kinds are:

🍎 Rhubarb and custard
🍎 Strawberry and raspberry
🍎 Apple and cinnamon
🍎 Chocolate chip and mint

So, how do I do it? I use a cheap, basic ice-cream maker to make simple, home-made ice cream using cream, sugar and fresh fruits.

For some of the more elaborate recipes you will need eggs, and you'll have to make a custard. However, for a basic, seriously scrummy ice cream, little time, cost or effort is required. It's worth keeping an eye out for a basic ice-cream maker. For very little money, your family can enjoy the delight of home-made ice cream. Think of the fun you will have concocting flavours. Really good ice cream can be quite expensive nowadays, so I think it's worth a small initial investment to be able to make your own. If I can do it, you can rest assured that it really is easy!

> 250g strawberries + 250ml cream + 125g caster sugar = strawberry ice-cream. For the full recipe, see page 115.

🍎 FREEZING FRUIT 🍏

On cold Sunday mornings in winter, I love to make pancakes for my family. Everyone piles around the table and helps themselves to pancakes drizzled with yoghurt and topped with our own home-grown raspberries or blackberries that were foraged during golden autumn days. In the depths of winter, it's hard to recall the sunny summer days when the raspberry bushes were laden with berries. As the autumn raspberries begin to fruit I start to freeze the crop, knowing it will make a truly welcome appearance on some dark, damp Sunday morning in mid-winter. Keep this in mind when your raspberries are fruiting and put some in the freezer to brighten up your winter.

Raspberries and blackberries are great for freezing. Unfortunately, whole strawberries never manage to make it to my freezer because they are simply too delicious to resist in the summer months. Some fruits might be slightly mushy when you defrost them, but the flavour will be retained.

Here's how I freeze my raspberries so some are still whole when they are defrosted:

- Pick the firmest raspberries for freezing (eat the softer fruits fresh).
- Wash and let them dry off on paper towels.
- Cover a tray with baking parchment and place the dry raspberries on the tray.
- Place the tray in the freezer and leave for a few hours until the raspberries are frozen.

🕯 Remove the tray, and bag and label the raspberries. Return the bagged raspberries to the freezer.

This method is very similar to the method for freezing herbs described in Chapter 2. I also use this method for foraged blackberries. These frozen fruits are ideal for making a delicious coulis or nutritious smoothie.

I also regularly stew apples throughout the fruiting season. Once they have cooled, I bag the stewed apple and put it in the freezer. Be sure not to freeze too much in one bag – you may just want to defrost a little for an apple sauce.

Rhubarb is easily frozen too and, together with some yogurt, makes a delicious topping for pancakes. Just remember to bag small amounts, as a little goes a long way with rhubarb.

To freeze rhubarb:

🕯 Take 5 stalks of rhubarb.
🕯 Wash and chop and place in a pot.
🕯 Add 50 mls water and simmer for 3–4 minutes, slightly softening the rhubarb, which should retain its shape.
🕯 Remove from the heat and allow to cool.
🕯 Place in a freezer bag, seal and freeze.
🕯 After defrosting the rhubarb, heat slowly and add sugar to sweeten to your taste.

☺ SO THERE YOU HAVE IT ... ☺

I hope you're feeling fruity after all that! When it comes to growing fruit the options are endless. I have tried to stick to what, in my experience, are good fruits to start off with. Although more expensive than packets of seeds, fruit bushes and trees can be a great investment. They also provide another wonderful way to teach children about where their food comes from – and that can only be a good thing.

Remember:

- ☺ Take it slowly.
- ☺ Mind your budget.
- ☺ Grow only what you like to eat.

So far we have looked at starting with herbs and filling windowsills with tomatoes. We have planned a lettuce supply that would make any rabbit proud. Potatoes in sacks, onions galore, strawberries in beds, raspberry bushes and apple trees – we've touched on growing these and lots more. But what about bringing them into the kitchen? The next chapter will give you an insight into my kitchen here at Hunters Lodge. Traditional, simple, fuss-free recipes that will nourish and soothe everyone in the household. Enjoy!

In The Kitchen –
Cooking and Home-Made Gifts

6

I F YOU'RE ANYTHING LIKE ME you probably have a stockpile of recipe books. Hundreds of variations of recipes for wholesome breads and succulent meats and every other dish you can think of. So what am I going to share with you that hasn't been written a hundred times before (and probably a hundred times better)?

I'm not a professional chef; I'm a good cook – well, at least my children think I am. Without labouring over the stove for hours, I've managed to put together a repertoire of recipes that are easy to make, not time consuming, and add a lovely traditional feeling to my cooking. Many of these recipes also make ideal gifts for friends and relatives. I'm just as busy in my daily life as you are, but it gives me a sense of comfort to know there's a cake in the tin or chutney in the larder, just like my grandmothers had. I hope these recipes will give you and your family that same feeling of comfort.

Modern appliances certainly do help make cooking easier, but by no means do I have the latest gadgets. I have a small food processor, a hand mixer and a small ice-cream maker. They probably cost less than €100 in total, but they work just fine.

BREAD AND CAKES

TRADITIONAL IRISH SODA BREAD

It takes only four ingredients to create this delicious white soda bread. More than any other bread, this is the bread that I recall from my youth. Visiting my father's parents in Offaly on a Sunday afternoon meant that by teatime my grandmother Isabella would be pulling freshly baked loaves from the oven. Served warm with leftover cold cuts from the Sunday roast and a mix of salads – it was truly a treat. It was a long time before I was to recreate that sensation in my own kitchen, but now not

a week goes by without a couple of loaves coming out of my own oven. It took me a long time to find the right mix of ingredients to make the bread just the way I like it, but now it's perfect every single time. It thrills me that my parents love this bread too because it brings back the exact same memories for them.

This recipe is so quick and simple that I often make some loaves in the morning before visiting friends later in the day. Wrapped up in parchment, it makes a great gift. It also freezes well, so I usually make two loaves at a time – one for eating and one for freezing. It's best eaten fresh, so if you will only eat half a loaf be sure to pop the other half in the freezer to keep it fresh till you need it.

Traditionally this bread is made with a cross on top of it. Some say it's the sign of the cross to ward off evil, while others will tell you it's simply to make it easier to share. Whatever the reason, I continue to mark a cross on top of all my soda bread loaves.

Ingredients (makes 1 loaf)

- 450 g plain flour
- 375 mls buttermilk
- 1 tsp salt
- 1½ tsp bread soda

You Will Need

- 1 large, non-stick baking tray
- Sieve
- Large bowl
- Wooden spoon
- Sharp knife
- Wire tray

Method

1. Preheat the oven to 200°C.
2. Lightly flour the baking tray.
3. Mix the flour, salt and bread soda together. Sieve into a bowl, then repeat the sieving process. This gives the bread an extra lightness.
4. Make a well in the centre of the flour and gradually add in the buttermilk, mixing slowly as the flour and milk come together. Some folks like to get in there and mix with their hands, but I use a wooden spoon.

5. When the mixture comes together in a ball, put the dough onto a floured board or worktop. The dough will be sticky, but two or three kneads on the floured board is all that is required. Putting a small bit of flour on your hands will prevent the dough from sticking to them. Once kneaded, shape the dough into a round loaf form. Place the bread onto the tray and, using a sharp knife, make two deep cuts across the bread to form a cross. I go right to the edge of the bread with these cuts.

6. Place the loaf in the centre of the oven and allow it to bake for 35–40 minutes. When you take the bread out, turn it over and tap the bottom of the bread. If it sounds hollow, your bread is ready.

7. Leave to cool on a wire tray.

8. Serve with home-made butter and jam (see recipes below) and a big pot of your favourite tea.

BROWN BREAD

When I'm cooking for my family, my recipes are dictated by whatever ingredients I have to hand. This means that recipes change slightly according to what fresh and store-cupboard ingredients are in the house at the time. It's a good way to ensure that there's no waste, and it saves time when I don't have to go shopping just for one ingredient.

This brown bread recipe is a good example of this. I interchange oats, bran and wheatgerm depending on what I have in the house. Because this is a very old recipe, I use pounds and ounces – over the years I have never converted it to grammes. Call me old-fashioned, but I don't want to change this one.

Ingredients

- Butter for greasing
- ½ lb plain flour
- ½ lb wholemeal flour – coarse
- 4 oz mixed oatmeal, bran or wheatgerm (whatever you have in the house)
- 1 tsp salt
- 1½ tsp bread soda
- 2 tsp sugar
- 1 tbsp sunflower oil
- ¾ pint buttermilk (you may need a little more if the mixture is too dry)

You Will Need

- 2 lb loaf tin
- Large bowl
- Wooden spoon, for mixing

Method

1. Preheat the oven to 200°C and grease the loaf tin.
2. Mix the dry ingredients together in a bowl.
3. Make a well in the centre and slowly add the buttermilk and oil while mixing together to form a dough.
4. Add more buttermilk if the dough is too dry.
5. Turn out onto a well-floured board and knead very lightly.
6. Put the dough in the greased tin and bake in the oven for 45 minutes.
7. Check that the bread is cooked by tapping the base for a hollow sound when you take it out of the oven. Allow to cool on a wire rack.

Optional

 You can add 1 tbsp of treacle to the buttermilk for a darker bread.

 Adding an egg to the buttermilk will give the bread a longer shelf life.

 When the dough is in the tin, sprinkle sesame seeds on top for extra texture.

 If you prefer a softer crust, cover the bread with a damp tea towel when it's removed from the oven.

ONE-STEP SPONGE CAKE

This is the recipe I use most often to make a basic sponge cake. There are tonnes of recipes out there that give a higher, lighter sponge, but I prefer this recipe for its simplicity. All you have to do is put four ingredients in a food processor, and you're done. So when you get that

call or text that says, 'Hi, we're passing by the door in an hour; are you home?' you can spend that hour tidying up and still manage to have a sweet treat for your guests. (I'm assuming you'd have to tidy up simply because it would be the first thing on my mind!)

The other reason I make this sponge is because it's deliciously dense, and our own duck eggs give it a rich golden colour. Hen eggs will work just as well. This method might be quick, but there's no compromising on taste.

Ingredients

- 3 large eggs
- 170 g soft margarine/ butter (chopped into 1-inch pieces)
- 170 g self-raising flour
- 170 g caster sugar
- Strawberry jam
- Whipped cream
- Icing sugar

You Will Need

- Two 8-inch sandwich tins
- Sieve
- Food processor
- Wire tray

Method

1. Preheat the oven to 200°C.
2. Grease the sandwich tins.
3. Put the first four ingredients into a food processor and mix for approximately 30 seconds to remove all the lumps.
4. Divide the mixture into the two tins and bake for 15 minutes.
5. Remove the cake halves from the tins and place on a wire tray to cool.
6. When the cake has cooled, place one half on a plate, spread with jam and top with cream. Spread jam on the second half and place on top of the first, jam side down. Sieve icing sugar over the cake to finish.

MADEIRA CAKE

'You'll have a bit of cake?' I'm sure you've heard that more than once in your lifetime. Those words are usually accompanied by the sound of a cake tin being opened and a Madeira cake or fruit cake appearing. Well, this is my version of a simple Madeira cake. Sometimes I add sultanas to it, sometimes cherries. But whether it's plain or with fruit, this buttery cake is great to have in the tin.

Ingredients

- 225 g softened butter (extra for greasing)
- 225 g caster sugar
- 4 eggs (beaten)
- 230 g self-raising flour (sifted)
- 50 g ground almonds
- 3 tbsp milk

You Will Need

- One 8-inch deep round cake tin
- Baking parchment
- Large bowl
- Hand mixer
- Wire tray

Method

1. Preheat the oven to 160°C. Grease and line the cake tin with parchment.

2. Beat the butter and sugar in a bowl using a hand mixer until the mixture is light and fluffy.

3. Gradually add in the eggs, then slowly fold in the flour and ground almonds.

4. Add enough milk to give the mixture a nice soft dropping consistency.

5. Pour the mixture into the prepared tin and bake in the oven for 75–90 minutes. When the cake has risen and is a golden colour, check that it's cooked thoroughly by inserting a skewer in the centre of the cake. If it comes out clean, your cake is done and you should remove it from the oven.

6. Leave the cake to cool in the tin for 15 minutes before turning it out onto a wire tray and removing the parchment.

7. Serve the cake when it has completely cooled, and store in an airtight container.

BREAKFAST AND BRUNCH

GRANOLA

'Real men don't eat granola, they eat muesli', according to Eamonn. Did you ever hear the likes of it? A raw mix of oats, nuts and seeds will give you a nutritious muesli, but add honey and sunflower oil to the same ingredients and bake in the oven and you've got yourself one fine home-made granola. And how could we stick to muesli when we have buckets of the finest honey right at our fingertips? So, Mr Dillon might like to say he eats muesli as part of his breakfast every morning, but we all know the truth!

This recipe is not only simple, but can be made according to whatever nuts and seeds you have in the cupboard. Because of this, no two batches are ever the same here at Hunters Lodge. Hazelnuts can be replaced with walnuts, and so on, and if we have both in the cupboard, well, we have a deliciously nutty granola to eat.

Make this granola when you have one hour to spare. It takes no time to put the ingredients together, but you must stir the mixture every five minutes or so during the hour it's in the oven to ensure it doesn't burn. I actually set a series of alarms for myself when the granola is in the oven – this way I am sure not to forget to turn it.

Ingredients

- 2 kg organic oats
- 400 g mixed nuts and seeds (walnuts, hazelnuts, sunflower seeds, linseed and pumpkin seeds, or any combination of these). Feel free to add more or less depending on the granola texture you like.
- 100 g dried fruits (optional)
- 150 mls sunflower oil
- ¾ jar local honey

You Will Need

- Medium-sized pot or saucepan
- Large baking or roasting tin
- Wire rack
- Air-tight container

Method

1. Preheat the oven to 150°C.
2. Warm the sunflower oil and the honey together slowly in a pot and remove from the heat.
3. In a large baking tin (a roasting tin is perfect) mix together the oats and whatever nuts and seeds you are using.

4. Pour over the oil and honey and mix thoroughly.
5. Place the tin in the oven for one hour, mixing the granola every 5–6 minutes while it's in the oven. Remember it is important that you check and mix the granola regularly while it is in the oven so it does not burn.
6. After one hour, remove the granola from the oven and allow it to cool completely on the wire rack.
7. At this point you can add your favourite dried fruits.
8. Store in an airtight container.
9. This makes a lovely gift. Just put some granola in an attractive jar and your friends will be thrilled with this home-made healthy jar of goodness.

BAKED EGGS

This is a weekend favourite here at Hunters Lodge and a great way to use our fresh eggs on a lazy Sunday morning. Using cheddar cheese and cream means it's not the healthiest of breakfasts, but once in a while we all deserve a treat like this. Add freshly baked soda bread, a pot of tea and the Sunday newspapers and you've got yourself the perfect lazy Sunday.

Ingredients (serves 4)
- Butter for greasing ramekins
- 200 g Irish cheddar (grated)
- 2 slices of ham (chopped)
- 4 large free-range eggs
- 150 ml cream
- Freshly ground black pepper

You Will Need
- 4 medium-sized ramekins

Method

1. Preheat the oven to 200°C.
2. Grease the four ramekins with the butter.
3. Divide half the cheese between the ramekins.
4. Layer the diced ham on top of the cheese.
5. Break an egg into each ramekin, then sprinkle with the remaining cheese and pour over the cream.
6. Lightly season with black pepper (this recipe does not require additional salt).
7. Bake for 15–20 minutes, until the eggs are set to your liking and the tops have browned.

SWEET TREATS

STRAWBERRY JAM

If you have a glut of strawberries, there's nothing nicer than making a fresh pot of home-made jam. This recipe is so simple, and not only can you and your family enjoy the delicious pleasure of home-made strawberry jam, but also your friends – they will be seriously impressed with a pot.

If you don't have enough strawberries on your windowsill or in your garden, don't let that put you off. Pick up some Irish strawberries at your local market or fruit and veg store and away you go.

Strawberries are low in pectin so I use jam sugar for this recipe, which guarantees me excellent results every time. Jam sugar is readily available in supermarkets.

Ingredients (makes 1 pot of jam)

- 225 g strawberries (washed, hulled and chopped)
- 225 g jam sugar
- ½ tsp of butter (a tip from my mother-in law)

You Will Need

- 350 ml sterilized jar and lid
- Oven-proof bowl
- Medium-sized pot or saucepan
- Wooden spoon
- Dessert spoon

Method

1. Put the sugar in a bowl and warm it in the oven (just warm it gently, don't let the sugar brown or crystallise).
2. Melt the butter in the pot and add the strawberries. Simmer over a low heat for about 3 minutes. While they're simmering, crush the strawberries a little to release their juices.
3. Add the warmed sugar and stir until the sugar is dissolved.
4. Increase the heat and bring the mixture to the boil. Once boiling, turn down the heat and let the mixture bubble gently for about 7–8 minutes.
5. In the meantime, put the dessert spoon in the freezer. After 7–8 minutes, remove the spoon from the freezer and drop a ¼ tsp of the jam onto the spoon. If it sets as it cools, your jam is ready. If not, continue to boil for up to 5 more minutes and repeat the testing process.
6. When you are happy with the consistency, remove your jam from the heat.
7. Take away any 'scum' that has formed on the top of the jam (it won't do you any harm but it doesn't look great).
8. Leave the jam to cool and set. Putting the jam into the jar while it is warm will cause the fruit to rise to the top.
9. When cooled, pour the jam into the sterilized jar and seal. If you are using a new lid there's no need to place a wax disc on top of the jam.

Make a simple soda bread (see recipe on page 98) to serve with this strawberry jam, and you'll bring the meaning of 'bread and jam' to a whole new level!

PERFECT PAVLOVA

If ever there was a reason to keep chickens in your garden, this is it.

I don't know about you, but I love a pavlova that is lightly crisp on the outside and gooey on the inside – that's my idea of heaven. I have perfected this recipe by trial and error over the years. I scanned cookery tomes and experimented continuously. Having an endless supply of eggs in the garden came in very handy, let me tell you. Now I have found my perfect pavlova. It's so easy to make that my daughter Ruth started making this herself when she was just 9 years old.

If you want a pavlova with a lovely gooey centre, take the meringue out of the oven as soon as it's cooked. If you prefer a crunchy meringue, leave it in the oven to cool.

I keep my pavlova simple. There are no added extras like vinegar, water or cornflour in this recipe. My method has simplicity written all over it, but the finished product will look totally amazing.

> It's very important that all the utensils you use when making your pavlova are spotlessly clean. The tiniest amount of grease or fat in your bowl will prevent the egg whites from stiffening.

Ingredients (makes 1 large pavlova, serves 8)

For the meringue
- 6 large free-range eggs
- 300 g caster sugar
- Pinch of salt

For the filling
- 350 ml cream
- 3 tbsp caster sugar to sweeten
- 300 g fruit of your choice.

Some of our favourite toppings include strawberries, raspberries, kiwis, grapes or bananas. You can include some or all of these, depending on your taste.

You Will Need
- Large baking tray
- Baking parchment
- Medium-sized bowl
- Hand mixer

Method
1. Preheat the oven to 150°C. Line the baking tray with parchment.
2. First, make the meringue. Separate the egg whites and put them in a bowl. Make sure there's no yolk or little bits of shell in there or your whites won't thicken. Whisk the egg whites until the mixture forms stiff peaks. I'm sure you know the classic method of checking to see if the mixture is thick enough – turn the bowl upside down over your head. If you're not covered in egg white, you're ready for the next step.
3. Add the sugar and salt and whisk for 3–4 minutes. When your mixture has a lovely glossy sheen and all the grainy pieces of sugar are gone, it's ready.
4. Spoon the mixture onto the parchment to make one large circular meringue. Alternatively, you can put spoonfuls of the mixture on the parchment to make individual meringues. Bake in the oven for 50 minutes or until crisp on the outside and gooey on the inside. Reduce oven time to 35 minutes for individual meringues.

5. When the meringue is cooked, remove it from the oven and leave it to cool.
6. To finish, top the meringue base with cream (sweeten the cream with the sugar if desired) and add your favourite fruits. For a banoffi effect, top the cream with bananas and drizzle with toffee sauce. Sprinkle with chocolate shavings to finish.

A good way to use up the leftover egg yolks from this recipe is to make some delicious custard. See my recipe below.

CREAMY CUSTARD

I have based this recipe on the amount of eggs required to make my pavlova (see recipe above), so basically a half dozen eggs will give you a fine big pavlova base (or two dozen meringues) and a pint of custard. Not bad!

Ingredients

- 400 ml milk
- 125 g caster sugar
- 1 tsp vanilla extract
- 6 egg yolks
- 1 tsp cornflour

You Will Need

- Medium-sized pot
- Whisk
- Large bowl
- Wooden spoon

Method

1. Heat the milk slowly in a pot and bring to the boil.
2. In a bowl, whisk together the egg yolks, vanilla extract and caster sugar until they become pale (2–3 minutes whisking by hand).
3. Add in the cornflour and mix thoroughly.
4. Pour the milk into the egg mixture, whisking as you pour. Whisk the eggs and the milk thoroughly. Pour the mixture into the pot and return to a low heat.

5. Stir continuously over a low heat until the custard starts to thicken. By the time the custard starts to bubble, it will have thickened sufficiently. Heating the custard too fast will cause the custard to split, so take your time.
6. Remove from the heat.
7. Serve immediately or allow to cool to use later.

LEMON POSSET

Waste not want not, I always say, and for cream that's just about to go out of date I have the perfect treat. I always seem to have a lemon lurking in the bottom of my fruit bowl towards the end of the week too, and with the addition of caster sugar these three ingredients will give you a quick-to-make and totally scrummy dessert. The kids love this one (probably because it's by no means healthy), but it also goes down a treat when served in a shot glass as part of a dessert plate for more discerning adults. Whether you dress it up or down, it is simply delightful, and my tried-and-tested method could not be easier.

Ingredients (makes 10 shot glasses)
- 300 mls double cream
- 70 g caster sugar
- Juice and zest of 1 large lemon

You Will Need
- Medium-sized pot
- 10 shot glasses

Method

1. Put the double cream in a pot with the sugar.
2. Bring *slowly* to the boil.
3. Reduce the heat and simmer for 3 minutes.
4. Remove the pot from the heat and add the lemon juice and zest.
5. Pour into glasses and refrigerate until set.

We are not zest fans here, so I normally just leave it out. Ginger or shortbread biscuits are perfect with this, and you can add a raspberry coulis topping for an extra burst of flavour if you wish.

Tea Loaf

I love this recipe for several reasons: it's a one-pot recipe, it freezes well, it tastes great, and it is the perfect excuse to enjoy some real country butter. Add a pot of tea, and we Dillons could not be happier!

Ingredients

- 225 g sultanas
- 225 g self-raising flour
- 115 g brown sugar
- 140 g butter
- 100 g cherries (chopped)
- 140 ml cold black tea
- 2 eggs (beaten)
- 1 tsp mixed spice
- 50 g chopped walnuts (optional)

You Will Need

- 2 lb loaf tin
- Baking parchment
- Medium-sized pot or saucepan
- Sieve
- Metal skewer or knife

Method

1. Preheat the oven to 190°C.
2. Grease and line the loaf tin with parchment.
3. Into the saucepan, put the sultanas, sugar, butter, tea, mixed spice, cherries and walnuts (if you are using them).

4. Bring to the boil, mixing thoroughly as the butter melts and the sugar dissolves.
5. Remove from the heat and allow to cool.
6. Add the eggs and then sieve and fold in the flour.
7. Pour the mixture into the loaf tin and bake for 55–60 minutes.
8. To test whether the cake is cooked, insert a metal skewer or a knife into the middle of the cake. If it comes out clean, your cake is ready.
9. Leave to cool before turning onto a wire tray.

SWEET STRAWBERRY ICE CREAM

Imagine picking juicy ripe strawberries in your garden on a warm summer's evening, knowing that you will use the fruit to make the finest ice cream for dessert the next day. With the help of an inexpensive ice-cream maker and my simple recipe, you can enjoy the most amazing home-made ice cream with minimal effort. For this basic recipe, you only need fruit, caster sugar and cream. No messing around with egg yolks and custards; this is the perfect way to start off your ice-cream-making journey.

Ingredients

- 250 g strawberries (washed and hulled)
- 250 mls cream
- 125 g caster sugar

You Will Need

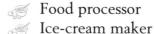

- Food processor
- Ice-cream maker

Method

1. Put the strawberries and caster sugar into the food processor and whizz.
2. Add the cream and whizz until mixed thoroughly with the strawberries.
3. Pour into your ice-cream maker and follow the manufacturer's instructions. This usually means churning the mixture for approximately 20–30 minutes until the mixture has formed an ice-cream consistency. Store in the freezer for up to six months.

I also use this recipe with raspberries, redcurrants (don't forget to sieve them), rhubarb (in the past I've used a spare jar of rhubarb and ginger compote) and apple and cinnamon (1 large cooking apple, stewed and cooled with 1 teaspoon of cinnamon). You can use this recipe to make a variety of very simple and utterly delicious ice creams before experimenting with more complicated custard-based ice creams in the future if you wish.

ROSEHIP SYRUP

Over the years I have developed the knack of producing decent food for the table, while spending the minimum of time in the kitchen, and quite often using the minimum of ingredients. Whether it's fresh bread or a beef stew, I don't compromise on taste or quality. Good quality ingredients will always speak for themselves. I'm always on the go so, quite honestly, it's a rare occasion that I indulge in hours and hours of prep and cooking time in the kitchen.

One of the best time-saving methods I have ever come across has to be this recipe for rosehip syrup, which is both delicious and a fantastic source of vitamin C. When I started making this syrup, I used the traditional method of boiling and straining and boiling some more. One would really wonder how much vitamin C is actually left in the syrup by the end of this process. These days I use a much simpler method. (For details on where to forage for rosehips, see Chapter 8.)

Ingredients

- Rosehips (freshly picked and washed) – you will need enough to fill the jar you're using three-quarters way

- White granulated sugar, enough to cover the rosehips

You Will Need
- Sterilized jam jar

Method
1. Wash and dry the rosehips, removing any bruised or old hips.
2. Fill the jar about three-quarters full with the rosehips.

3. Cover the rosehips with sugar until you can no longer see the hips if looking down into the jar. Seal the jar tightly.
4. Store in a dark cupboard and shake every day to ensure the sugar dissolves.
5. When the sugar has completely dissolved (in about 10–14 days), your syrup is ready. Super easy! Just remember that this may contain a slight amount of alcohol due to the sugar fermenting.
6. Strain through a muslin cloth before use.

It is very important to ensure that both the jar and the lid are spotlessly clean and airtight, or mould will develop very quickly. Rosehip syrup does not have a very long shelf life, but with a sterile jar it will last long enough to see you through the worst of the winter.

Cool Ice Pops

There's nothing more thirst-quenching on a sunny day than a home-made ice lolly packed with the taste of your favourite fruits. Strawberry, raspberry, lemon, blackberry, orange, the list goes on and on. Ice-pop cases are readily available, inexpensive and reusable, so pick up a few the next time you see them. Feel free to adjust these recipes to suit your own taste – add more sugar for more sweetness or reduce the sugar for a tangier taste. Play around with them until you have found your favourites, then keep a stash in your freezer.

Some ice lolly recipes require ingredients to be heated in a pot to dissolve the sugar. However, I simply boil the kettle for hot water and use it to dissolve the sugar (which means there's no pot to clean).

Orange and Lemon Pops
Ingredients

You Will Need

- 2 oranges and 1 lemon
- 100 mls hot water
- 100 g caster sugar

- Medium-sized bowl or jug
- Sieve
- Ice-pop cases

Method

1. Squeeze the oranges and lemon to give you approximately 150 mls of juice.

2. Strain if necessary to remove pips, etc.
3. Dissolve the sugar in the hot water and add the juice.
4. Pour into ice-pop cases and freeze until ready to use.

Real Raspberry Lollies

Ingredients

- 125 g fresh raspberries
- 75 g caster sugar
- 250 mls hot water

You Will Need

- Medium-sized bowl or jug
- Food processor
- Sieve
- Ice-pop cases

Method

1. Place the raspberries in a food processor and whizz until smooth.
2. If you like, you can strain the mixture now, but I don't bother. I love the texture of all the 'bits'.
3. Dissolve the sugar in the hot water and add to the raspberries. Whizz together in the food processor for a couple of seconds.
4. Pour the mixture into ice-pop cases and freeze until you need them.

SWEET AND SOUR CUCUMBER PICKLE (BREAD AND BUTTER PICKLE)

There are millions of cucumber pickle recipes out there. My fellow food bloggers have been so helpful throughout the years when it comes to turning those cucumbers into a delectable accompaniment for meats and sandwiches. All the recipes I tried tasted great, but I particularly love the ones that have a long shelf life. Long after all the cucumbers have been harvested, and way before the barbeque season begins, this pickle recipe, which is packed with punch, will liven up any food on the dullest of days. I've played around to get the flavour that I like – give it a go and feel free to change it to your own taste.

Ingredients

- 400 g cucumbers (finely sliced)
- 250 g onions (finely sliced)
- 250 mls apple cider vinegar
- 180 g sugar
- 30 g salt
- ½ tbsp mustard seeds

You Will Need

- Bowl
- Sieve
- Medium-sized pot
- 4 sterilized jam jars

Method

1. Put the cucumber and onions in a bowl and sprinkle with the salt.
2. Leave to stand for a few hours, then rinse well and strain.
3. Put the vinegar, sugar and mustard seeds into a pot and bring to the boil. Simmer for 4–5 minutes.
4. Remove from the heat and add the cucumbers and onions.
5. Return to the heat and bring to the boil. As soon as boiling point has been reached, remove the pot from the heat and pour the mixture into the sterilized jars.
6. Leave for at least six weeks before eating.

TOMATO RELISH

No larder would be complete without this. An easy-to-make tomato chutney that is guaranteed to bring the most boring sandwich to life. This recipe makes two small jars, so double the ingredients if you would like to have something in the cupboard for that last-minute gift. If you like your relish hot, spice things up by adding chilli to the mix.

Ingredients

- 500 g tomatoes
- 130 g cooking apples
- 130 g onions
- 100 g brown sugar
- 30 g sultanas
- 150 mls apple cider vinegar
- ¼ tsp ground ginger
- ¼ tsp ground cloves
- ¼ tsp chilli flakes (optional)

You Will Need

- 2 small, sterilized jars
- Medium-sized pot

Method

1. Mix all the ingredients in a pot and simmer until the mixture has thickened (this will take about two hours at a very low heat).
2. Pour the relish into the jars and seal.
3. Leave in your cupboard/larder for at least four weeks before using.

Pea Soup

What is a garden without peas, I ask you. How anyone could deprive themselves of such a delicious snack while out in the garden I don't know. Unless of course you don't like peas. We like them so much here that it's hard to keep a stockpile in the freezer. Frozen peas from the supermarket are the next best thing if you don't have a glut of your own peas. Pea soup is quick, economical and easy to make. Served with homemade bread, it makes a vibrant, tasty lunch.

Ingredients

- 450 g fresh or frozen peas
- 4 shallots (diced) or 1 onion (diced)
- 2 leeks (diced)
- 1 potato (peeled and chopped)
- 25 g butter
- 800 mls vegetable stock
- Salt and pepper to season

You Will Need

- Medium-sized pot
- Food processor or liquidizer

Method

1. Melt the butter and add the shallots and leeks. Stir over a low heat for a couple of minutes until they start to soften.
2. Add the potato and cook for one minute.

3. Add the peas and the stock and bring to the boil.
4. Reduce the heat and simmer for 25 minutes.
5. Allow to cool for 15 minutes.
6. Pour the soup into a food processor or liquidizer and process until it's smooth.
7. Return to the pot and reheat gently.
8. Season to taste, and serve.

TOM'S SPUD AND SCALLION SOUP

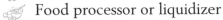

Could you get a more Irish soup than this? Ridiculously easy to make and seriously tasty. And who is Tom, you might ask. Tom Nolan and his wife, Mary, live about two miles away from us, and kinder people you couldn't meet. I bought my first chickens from Tom many years ago, and over the years we have become great friends. My parents need never worry about me while I have Tom and Mary looking out for me. They are kindred spirits really, with a garden full of poultry just like mine.

Tom is always calling me when he has a glut of something – scallions, tomatoes, anything really. This recipe came about after I got a call to say he had surplus scallions and spuds.

Ingredients (serves two)

- 30 g butter
- 6 scallions (topped, tailed and chopped)
- 2 medium potatoes (peeled and diced)
- 500 ml vegetable stock
- Salt and pepper to season

You Will Need

- Medium-sized pot or saucepan
- Food processor or liquidizer

Method

1. Melt the butter in a saucepan.
2. Add the scallions and cook for one minute, stirring all the time.
3. Add the diced potatoes and stir for another minute.
4. Add the stock and bring to the boil, then simmer on a low heat for 20 minutes.
5. Remove from the heat and allow to cool slightly.
6. Liquidize the soup until it is smooth, or leave some potato pieces in if you prefer.
7. Season to taste, and serve.

Our Dublin Dinner (Beef Casserole Cooked in a Slow Cooker)

My school years were spent in Galway, and I have many fond memories of weekends spent on the beach in Bearna. Of course, the sun always seemed to be shining, and I can't think of egg and tomato sandwiches or Coke without being transported right back to that beach. Back then, it wasn't unusual for us all to be piled into the car on a Friday evening, and we would head to Dublin for the weekend. From the time I was little, I absolutely adored my grandmother Stella. She was a kind, gentle lady, with a great sense of fun. I loved her very much. When she died, I thought the pain would never leave my heart. The pain of course eased over time, but my fond memories of her are still as vivid as ever. I try to keep one particular memory of my grandmother alive by sharing it with my own children – Dublin dinner. Actually, it's simply a beef casserole, but Granny Stella served it with doorsteps of white bread and lashings of butter. As youngsters, my sisters and I used to ask, 'Can we have our Dublin dinner today?' and my mother knew exactly what we were talking about. Today, my own children love my Dublin dinner. When I first made this casserole for Eamonn, it transported him back to his own youth and memories of his grandmother making something similar. To preserve the traditional taste of my grandmother's casserole, I use shin beef in this recipe – an old cut of beef that went out of fashion, but in reality it's packed with flavour and very economical.

My grandmother's trick for a lovely thick gravy was that old favourite, Bisto.

Ingredients

- 1 lb shin beef (diced)
- 2 onions (diced)
- 2 sticks of celery (diced)
- 8 carrots (roughly chopped)
- 1 l beef stock
- 5 tbsp flour
- 4 tbsp Bisto
- 1 tbsp Worcestershire sauce
- Salt and pepper to season
- Oil for frying
- 100 mls water

You Will Need

- A large bowl
- Frying pan
- Slow cooker or casserole dish

Method

1. Mix the flour and Bisto together in a bowl. Season with salt and pepper.
2. Add the meat to the bowl and mix until it gets a good coating of flour.
3. Heat the oil in a pan and add the beef, small batches at a time. Remove from the pan when browned thoroughly and place in the slow cooker.
4. If you have flour remaining in the bowl, add the water to form a paste.
5. Add the vegetables, stock and Worcestershire sauce to the meat. Mix in the flour paste thoroughly.
6. Slow cook for 4–5 hours, or as per your slow cooker instructions. If you don't have a slow cooker, don't worry, just use your oven at a low temperature (150°C). Place your casserole in any dish with a tight lid, and this will work perfectly.
7. Serve with freshly baked bread for a heart-warming, comforting family dinner.

A LITTLE BITTA BUTTER

Up until recently I would have laughed uproariously if anyone had suggested that I make my own butter. I'm all for traditional skills, but butter-making? No thank you. I love the simple life, but butter-making sounded complicated. One day, however, I saw a butter-making recipe

in a book, and the method used involved shaking cream in a plastic milk carton until you had butter. Well, of course, I had to give it a go. And the result? A disastrous, gucky mess that I promptly threw out. I was intrigued about where I had gone wrong though, so I did some research. This recipe is the result of my research and subsequent experimenting. I don't have access to raw cream,

so I buy double cream to make butter. This certainly isn't a cost-saving exercise, but it's worth the small effort required to produce fantastic gifts of home-made butter.

Ingredients

- 500 mls double cream
- Salt (if desired)

You Will Need

- 3 spotlessly clean bowls
- Hand mixer
- Ice-cold water
- Sieve

Method

1. First things first – run cold water over your hands to cool them down. You will have to handle the butter in this process, and cool hands will help keep the butter firm as you shape it.
2. Ensure your bowls are spotlessly clean and cold.
3. Pour the cream into a bowl and whip using your hand mixer on a medium speed. Once the cream has thickened, continue to whip for another few minutes. Very quickly the cream will break down, and you'll notice two things – your cream has turned to butter and buttermilk is seeping from it into the bottom of the bowl.
4. Put the butter into the sieve and allow any excess buttermilk to drain off. Catch this buttermilk in a bowl or jug, as it is perfect for making soda bread (see recipe on page 98).
5. Place the butter in a clean bowl and beat with the mixer to release any more buttermilk that is remaining.
6. Place the ice cold water in the third bowl and add the butter. Gently knead it to release any remaining buttermilk. Drain the water and repeat the process a couple more times until the water is clear. Now your butter is ready to be shaped whatever way you like.
7. If you are using salt, add it just before you shape your butter. You will need ¼ tsp salt per 115 g of butter. Spread the butter on a clean board, sprinkle the salt across it and mix it in with a cool knife. When the salt is mixed through, shape the butter.
8. Wrap the butter in parchment paper and keep it chilled in the fridge.

Top Tips:
- Keeping all your utensils and your hands cool is very important when making butter.
- Rinsing the butter well gives you a longer-lasting butter.
- Adding salt gives the butter a shelf life of a couple of weeks.

🍎 ADULTS ONLY 🍎

RASPBERRY GIN/VODKA

Your guests will be more than impressed when you produce an exquisite home-made raspberry gin or vodka when they next call round for a get-together. I always have a bottle of each in the larder and love to serve it with cucumber ice cubes (juice a cucumber, put the juice in ice cube trays and freeze).

Ingredients
- 70 cl bottle of either gin or vodka
- 180 g raspberries (it's okay to use your stash from the freezer)
- 165 g granulated sugar

You Will Need

 Large Kilner jar or something similar that's clean with a good seal

Method

1. Place the gin or vodka, raspberries and sugar in the jar and shake.
2. Put a label on the back of the jar with the date and the amount of each ingredient used. This is a good reference if you want to adjust the sweetness, fruitiness, etc. to suit your taste.
3. Shake once a day for about a week or so until the sugar has completely dissolved.
4. Place in your larder/cupboard for about six weeks before drinking. You can taste it after four weeks and add more sugar if you like. Remember to make a note of it on the label if you add more sugar so you know how much to use next time.

SLOE GIN/VODKA

I'm not one to boast, but I'm putting it out there now that I make the best sloe gin this side of the Mississippi! A fine statement to make, I hear you say, but really you can't go wrong with sloe gin. This is our Christmas drink. Made in the autumn with foraged sloes, this glorious liquid will warm the cockles of your heart on the coldest of winter days. It matures beautifully over the years, if you can wait that long. (See Chapter 8 for tips on foraging for sloes.)

You don't need to use an expensive bottle of gin or vodka for this recipe. Any decent bottle will do.

Ingredients

- 250 g sloes
- 125 g granulated sugar
- 70 cl gin (or vodka)

You Will Need

- A freezer bag
- 1 large Kilner jar (1-litre capacity)

Method

1. Wash and dry the sloes.
2. Place the sloes in a freezer bag and pop them into the freezer until they are frozen. The reasons for doing this are twofold:

1) the freezer replicates a natural frost, which slightly sweetens the sloes, and 2) the sloes will burst when frozen, which allows their distinctive flavour to penetrate the alcohol.

3. Remove the sloes from the freezer and put them in the Kilner jar. Add the sugar and top with the gin or vodka.

4. If you want to use fresh sloes, prick each sloe before you put it in the jar so that the flavour will be released.

5. Leave the jar on your kitchen worktop for a week and shake it a couple of times a day. The liquid will gradually turn to a deep pink colour, and the sugar will dissolve. When the week is up, remove the jar to your larder and leave it for at least eight weeks, giving it a shake every so often to ensure the sugar has completely dissolved. Some people like to remove the sloes, but as long as there's still alcohol in the jar, I leave the sloes where they are.

6. Decant into smaller gift bottles for Christmas gifts (to over 18s, naturally).

THE GIFT OF GIVING

I've certainly gone back to basics when it comes to giving gifts. When did it happen that you had to go to a shop to buy wine, chocolates or flowers before visiting somebody's house? Why did it become almost compulsory to do this? Was it simply a time issue? Or did we just have too much money? Well, most of us certainly don't have too much money nowadays. But that doesn't mean that you can't have a richness of gifts to give friends. Throughout this book I hope you will have come across many ideas for gifts, most of them costing you hardly anything. Gifts, naturally, will vary depending on the occasion. There's the thank you gift for a teacher, the gift for a dinner-party host, the birthday gift for a friend or relative, to name but a few. Here are some of the gifts I like to give to my friends and loved ones:

129

Fresh soda bread	Irish toffee	Jar of honey
Fresh eggs	Pot of herbs	Home-made sausages
Chocolate cake	Raspberry gin	Tomato relish
Sloe gin	Cucumber pickle	Home-made butter

All these gifts are home-made and very well received, let me assure you. In fact, people often ask me before I visit to bring my bread or relish with me, depending on what they prefer. Some of the gifts are simply growing in the garden and require hardly any effort from me to prepare. Others, like the bread, are quick and easy to make. Having pickles and chutneys in the cupboard or larder not only means that I get to enjoy them myself, but also that I have access to gifts whenever I need them.

Apart from sloe gin at Christmas, and raspberry gin by special request, I'm inclined to leave the likes of home-made cider, wine and mead for consumption here at Hunters Lodge. Friends come over and love to try them, but I just don't like to impose our concoctions on an unassuming host, especially if I'm not sure of the alcohol content. But that's just me.

Although I personally love home-made gifts, I'm not saying you should never buy your friends a nice bottle of wine or some hand-made chocolates. I could certainly see my own friends heading into the distance if I felt like that. I'm simply saying that you have options – alternatives that are likely to cost less and possibly mean more. Whether money is an issue or not, it is nice to put some thought into a gift, and people will appreciate the effort you have made.

RECYCLING AND UPCYCLING

Just because you are not spending money does not mean your gift cannot look beautiful. Start keeping a little stash of string, pretty fabrics and greaseproof paper (great for breads and home-made butter). Recycle or 'upcycle' milk cartons and cream cartons to make cute little baskets for hen and quail eggs. Watch out for end-of-season sales at homeware and department stores where you often find small wicker baskets at seriously knock-down prices. These make excellent presentation baskets for special occasions. Sometimes you don't need an occasion; it's just nice to give somebody a gift.

It is also a great idea to start keeping glass jars, especially pretty ones. I use these jars for my everyday jams and chutneys. However, if I'm making a stash of chutneys, etc. for the larder that may be given to friends at a later date, I use brand new jars. This isn't strictly necessary, but I like to do it. Plain jam jars are not expensive to buy. Nowadays, I bulk buy my lids. These are inexpensive, and I use new lids on my everyday goodies and those for the larder.

> If you can't grow or bake your own gifts, try the next best thing and buy some local produce to give as a gift. By buying local cheese, honey and breads, you are supporting your local community.

WHAT'S NEXT?

As you can see, it's not terribly difficult to give your food and gifts that lovely 'home-made feeling'. The smell of soda bread baking in your kitchen, topping your burgers with a crunchy pickle or having a cake in the tin will fill your heart with delight and your tummy with goodies similar to those enjoyed by generations before us.

But if you already keep a few chickens, grow your own vegetables and put them all to good use in the kitchen, what's next? I'm asked this question more and more frequently, which can only be a good thing. The following chapter is all about taking the next step on your back-to-basics journey. It offers tips and advice for those considering raising meat for the table or keeping bees.

The Next Step

7

ONE OF THE BIGGEST (and most pleasant) surprises I've had over the years was that the more food I grew, the more I wanted to grow. After successfully growing fruit, vegetables, potatoes and tomatoes, I began to explore other options. I wondered whether it would be possible to rear meat in the garden and, if it was, I asked myself whether I'd be able for it. Would I become attached to the bird/animal? Would I have to kill it myself? Rearing meat for the table is not a decision to be taken lightly. There was a lot of thinking to be done. And not just about meat – were there other food options out there for me?

This chapter may not be for everyone. I was keeping chickens for ten years before I finally made the decision to rear birds for the table. So maybe it's not for you right now, but you never know what the future may hold.

When I embarked on my back-to-basics food journey, I'll admit to fantasizing about keeping a couple of pigs in the garden. It was like I instinctively knew that this was the right path to take. But what did I know about pigs? Zilch! Chickens I knew a lot about, but there was no way that the chickens I already had were heading to the table. Eating Daisy, Robbie, Boxcar Willie and George was absolutely not an option. Some of them were good dual-purpose breeds (good for eggs and the table), but it just wasn't going to happen. And as for Mahatma Gander and Willow Goose? Not a chance! That was like considering rearing our little dog Pippi for the table. No, this plan to rear meat was going to take a lot of consideration, research, soul-searching and practical planning. So that's what I did. Today, we enjoy our own free-range chicken, duck and turkey, and the finest pork, ham, sausages and rashers, as well as many other cuts of pork and bacon. Not bad for a garden!

As well as meat, we enjoy our own honey thanks to our bees that reside at the very end of the garden. While I'll admit that initially it was I who had the madcap idea to keep bees, nowadays Eamonn is very much the head beekeeper here at Hunters Lodge. Thanks to his quiet dedication and to the industrious bees themselves, we have been self-sufficient in honey for some years now. For this I am truly grateful.

But there's always a next step for everyone, and for me it's to get a goat. I have had that hankering (like I had for pigs) for quite some time now. The only thing stopping me is time. I'm not sure if I can commit to milking a goat every day. Before deciding to rear an animal you must give it plenty of consideration. In the meantime, I visit a neighbour's farm to milk one of his goats. This allows me to make my own yoghurt and, for the moment, I am very happy with this arrangement.

The one thing I will say before I go any further is that a good, decent-sized freezer is really important if you want to rear your own meat. When you dispatch your animals (slaughter them for meat), it's likely that you will have enough meat for more than one meal, so your freezer becomes your best friend. I keep mine in the garage and, very often, my version of going to the supermarket is actually going to the freezer.

 QUAIL

Let's say you have a few chickens and you want to try something new. I hear this quite a bit at my classes, and I always recommend quail. Not for the table, but for eggs. You know how expensive quail eggs can be, and it really is so easy to have your own supply. You can buy a female quail for less than €10. Once they have twelve hours daylight, they lay like there's no tomorrow. They require very little space and, being so small, their food bill is very low. If you enjoy quail eggs, this is definitely the way to go – and hard boiled, they are great for little lunch boxes.

BROILERS

They may be the quickest way to rear meat, but I had always dismissed broilers as an option for the table. My image of these chickens was that they were lazy, dirty and smelly. They would eat all day and keel over from a heart attack if I wasn't careful. In the main, broilers have all their foraging instincts bred out of them, so they are happy to eat all day and put on weight without any interest in the great outdoors. Great for big, fat roast chickens, but not so great for me or the birds themselves. There had to be another way. After careful research I came across a breed of broilers called Wessex Supreme. These birds still retain some of their foraging instincts, and they have worked out very well for me. I don't rear them intensively, and they spend their days foraging and basking in sunshine with all the other birds.

You could rear purebreds like Light Sussex for the table but, personally, I find I can't disassociate myself from those birds like I can with broilers. It doesn't mean that I treat the broilers any differently but, in my head, they are there for one purpose and that is for the table. This way I can be kind to them and rear them well but without getting too attached. And you don't want to get attached, because these birds have to be dispatched.

If you are considering rearing birds for the table do not buy them until you have a dispatching plan in place. You need to be well informed if you are going to do the job yourself, or have made arrangements with somebody to do the job for you. When it comes to dispatching, there are some important points to remember:

- Do not feed the bird for 24 hours before dispatching, but do allow them a supply of water.
- After the bird has been killed, pluck it immediately while it is still warm.
- Hang the bird for approximately three days to tenderise the meat.

- After the hanging process, the bird's innards can be cleaned out.
- In some parts of the country, there are processing plants that will carry out the dispatching and cleaning processes for you.

Like I said earlier, I was a poultry keeper for ten years before I decided to take this step. When I taste my home-reared chicken, I wish I had done it earlier.

TALKING TURKEY

Rearing a turkey for Christmas is becoming hugely popular. When you consider the savings to be made for a superb free-range turkey, it's not that surprising. If you are already keeping chickens, I'm sure this has crossed your mind – and it's not that difficult. Like broilers, be sure you have a dispatch plan in place before you proceed. You have no idea of the amount of emails and calls I get every December when it's time to dispatch the birds. There are a lot of turkeys successfully reared in this country with nobody to dispatch them for Christmas. Please don't make this mistake. Don't presume your butcher will do it for you because more than likely they won't.

We don't breed turkeys here at Hunters Lodge, so each autumn we buy a few turkey poults to rear for Christmas and the freezer. I buy mine from reputable breeders in my area. We usually pay in the region of €15 for a 6–8-week-old poult. White turkeys (I call them the broiler version of turkeys) are the most widely available, with Bronze turkeys also being a popular choice. We have reared both in the garden, and the meat from both was equally flavoursome (with the Bronze being slightly more gamey). When it comes to plucking, we have found that White turkeys are by far the easiest to pluck.

Now it's confession time: the first time we reared three turkeys I was afraid that they would have no meat on them by Christmas week. As we were rearing one for a friend, this concerned me greatly. I didn't want to be responsible for another family looking at their turkey on Christmas day without a sign of meat on it. So I didn't give the birds any fruit, vegetables or grain. I stuck rigidly to their diet of growers and finishers – 'growers' being pellets containing the correct amount of protein and nutrients to help the bird grow and 'finishers' being the pellets that would 'fatten up' the bird. By the time they were ready to be dispatched, the three turkeys weighed 34 lbs, 36 lbs and 37 lbs, respectively. Too big for the oven! So learn from my mistakes. It's okay to give your turkeys fruit, vegetables and grain. They will enjoy the variety in their diet and will continue to put on weight.

Ideally, your turkeys should be housed separately to any chickens you may have. If they are living and running in a small space with chickens they may be susceptible to a parasite called Blackhead, which could be fatal. Here at Hunters Lodge, the turkeys have separate housing, but they do free-range in the garden with the other birds without any problems.

If you are considering raising turkeys, bear the following in mind:

- Have a dispatch plan in place before buying your turkeys.
- Turkeys should have their own housing.
- Fresh bedding is essential, particularly if your turkeys are not roosting.
- Withdraw food 24 hours before dispatch, but allow a supply of water.
- Allow the turkey to hang for at least five days to tenderise the meat before cleaning it out.
- As with all animals, buy at least two turkeys so the birds have company.

When it comes to dispatching, turkeys are big birds, and you will need some strength. Allow plenty of time for not only dispatching but plucking too. Put on your favourite music and the plucking time will fly by – no pun intended!

Finally, enjoy the truly excellent flavour of your own garden-reared turkey. You really can't beat it.

🍎 DALLYING WITH DUCKS 🍐

Ducks are probably the cutest and most entertaining of all backyard animals. Watching them waddling across the lawn, quacking to their hearts' content, is most entertaining. They have great personalities and are a great addition to any garden. But they're not called mucky ducks for nothing. Ducks love water, and they love turning the ground into mud.

> Water source + ducks = mud!

Given the amount of rain we have in this country, ducks that have access to your garden will happily transform wet areas of grass into mini-swamps. If you have a spare field to let them wreak havoc in that's great, but allowing them to free-range in your garden can be a different matter entirely. But this is really the only negative and, if you manage the situation properly, there's no reason why you can't keep a couple of ducks while retaining your lawn in reasonable condition. In the winter, my ducks are enclosed in a run that allows them plenty of access to water in an area that is away from the main garden. There, they can create as many muddy puddles as they like. Once the grass begins to grow, I give them access to the garden once again.

Duck eggs enjoy something of a mixed reputation. Some people love them, others wouldn't touch them for love nor money. It doesn't help that given half a chance a duck will lay on muddy ground, which is never appealing. Duck eggs are also often associated with salmonella. Personally, I wouldn't dream of baking a cake without using duck eggs. They are well documented as the egg of choice for bakers. But there are some basic rules to follow when using duck eggs:

- Always ensure that the egg is cooked thoroughly.
- Do not lick a spoon or baking bowl that has been used to make a mixture with raw duck eggs.
- Do not give/sell duck eggs without complying with all Department of Agriculture regulations. See www.agriculture.gov.ie for more details.

Ideally, you should house your ducks separately from your chickens. If you would like to test your flock for salmonella, there are centres across Ireland that will test swab samples for you.

Apply the same principles for rearing chickens for the table to your ducks. But be warned – plucking ducks is much more difficult than plucking chickens.

A TALE OF TWO PIGS

Why I always wanted two pigs in the garden I do not know. It wasn't like I grew up with pigs or had any first-hand experience of them. I know my family and friends are sometimes at a loss for words when they hear my plans, but the idea of pigs just wouldn't go away no matter how often they threw their hands in the air despairingly. If it was at all possible, what could be so wrong with having a supply of pork and bacon directly from the garden? I toyed with the idea of hiring some land for two pigs, but the concept of renting a field went against my philosophy to grow and rear in my own garden. I abandoned that thought after serious deliberation and started to think about how I could make the plan work within the garden. I started doing some research and, no more than with the chickens, people had lots of comments to make about pig-rearing, many of them valid. What about the smell? What about cleaning them out? What if they got out into the garden? The list went on and on. One step at a time, I dealt with all eventualities with lots of help and advice from local Department of Agriculture vets. I followed all the building, space and safety regulations and, before I knew it, I was officially a pig farmer.

We love rearing pigs here. They are the most sociable of creatures and extremely easy to love. This makes parting with them very hard, but I remind myself of the alternative. A lot of the pork and bacon in our butchers and supermarkets comes from intensively reared pigs. To the best of my knowledge, intensively reared pigs do not enjoy fresh fruit every day. They don't have their fat bellies scratched until they fall over in ecstasy. They don't get to root in a mud bath and fall into a deep slumber half buried in fresh straw. Our pigs might not have an acre to run around in, but they are very lucky. And I can't think of a better form of food education for our children. They have huge respect for these lovely animals. They understand wholly and completely where their meat is coming from. They appreciate the time and the effort that goes into rearing a happy, healthy animal and, believe me, they have seen enough pig antics here in the garden to keep their own children entertained with plenty of anecdotes and stories in years to come.

While I was a complete novice when it came to pig-rearing, Eamonn's family had kept pigs at the back of their grocery shop in Bagenalstown, County Carlow when he was young. It's funny how quickly all the memories came flooding back to him when we got our first two piglets. Every evening when he came home from work the first thing he would ask was, 'How are the girls?' No, not his daughters – the pigs! We often find him in the pig run first thing on a Saturday morning cleaning out the house and putting in fresh straw for his 'girls' or 'the boys', depending on what we have at the time. Like I say, our pigs may not have an acre to run around in, but they are definitely the lucky ones.

Over the past couple of seasons, I have noticed a marked increase in the interest in pig-rearing at my classes. People are curious to see first-hand what it's like to rear pigs for the table. If pig-rearing is something you might be interested in, the following information should assist you:

- It is illegal to keep pigs in Ireland without a 'pig herd number', even if you're just keeping a couple of pigs in your back garden. Whether it's two or two hundred, you must have a herd number. Even if you have applied for a number, it is illegal to purchase your pigs until a number has been designated to you. You will find the application form on the Department of Agriculture website (www.agriculture.gov.ie). After you have submitted the form, your premises will be inspected before you are allocated a number.
- As with all animals, you must have safe, dry housing for your pigs. The guidelines for run sizes are available from the Department of Agriculture. We built a brick house for our pigs, but this is not necessary. Any secure shelter that provides adequate space and protection from the elements should suffice. It goes without saying, but secure fencing is a must. I personally do not like to use electric fencing, which is why we built a brick wall to contain our pigs. The gate area allows the pigs to see what's going on in the garden. Believe it or not, this is important, as they really do seem to enjoy watching the chickens and ducks meandering across the lawn.
- Your pigs will require a constant source of fresh drinking water.
- We decided to concrete part of the area in the pig run to make cleaning/feeding easier and left another part for the pigs to root around in. The pigs really enjoy this area where they can root away in the muck to their hearts' content.

- It is a good idea to have a compost area near the pig run to dispose of waste. We constructed a compost area right beside the pig run for ease of use.
- Our pigs are fed on a diet which is almost entirely fruit and veg.
- Before applying for your herd number, consider your options when it comes to taking your pigs to the abattoir. Have you had any recommendations for abattoirs in your area? Can you take a trailer directly to the gate of your pig run? Will you be able to physically and mentally take your pigs to be slaughtered? Abattoir day is a terrible day for me. Don't think that it's going to be easy. Think carefully about this before you buy pigs. If you decide it's not for you, at least you've made the right decision for you. If you decide to proceed, there's no doubt that you will not only enjoy top-class pork and bacon, but a wonderful life experience.
- Finally, simply because you have a pig herd number doesn't mean that you can now buy a goat or a sheep. You must apply for a separate herd number if you would like to keep either goats or sheep in your garden.

BUSY BEES

I might have longed to have pigs in the garden but never in my wildest dreams did I consider becoming a beekeeper. Eamonn and I both agree that, even in ten years' time, we will still consider ourselves novice beekeepers, such is the complexity of beekeeping.

I suppose beekeeping is slightly different to raising poultry and other animals in that most people associate bees with pain. I certainly didn't want to get stung, and I dreaded the day it would happen. In actual fact I have only been stung once (on my face, of course), and it was entirely my own fault. So my record is quite good. Eamonn, on the other hand, has had more stings than I and, unfortunately, we discovered that he is slightly allergic to bee stings. Not life-threatening allergic, but his hand or face will swell up after a sting. So he is particularly careful and

rarely gets stung nowadays. But, believe me, the threat of a sting in no way keeps us away from our hives.

The hours pass by unnoticed when tending to bees. It's like a form of therapy. You need to be calm, relaxed and take your time with bees. The hours just flit away, and at the end of it all you are rewarded with the most glorious honey you can imagine. Sometimes it tastes of our crab-apple trees, sometimes wild blackberries. But it's always delicious. For us, it is a true privilege to have honey from our own bees.

If you want to keep bees, start the process by enrolling in a beekeeping course for beginners in your area. This is the single most important piece of advice that I can give you about beekeeping. Don't be tempted to get started because you have been given an old hive and somebody has offered you a colony of bees. Get off to a good start with an introductory course and take it from there. You will learn about good husbandry, common ailments and the benefits of accurate record-keeping. More importantly, you will get to speak with experienced beekeepers, and their knowledge really is invaluable. Ideally,

locate and make contact with an experienced beekeeper in your area. You'll find that they are more than likely very willing to help you.

Most courses include a trip to an apiary, and, if you have had no experience of working with bees, this will be your test. I remember my first visit. Off we went, myself and five male students on our first visit to an apiary. Can you imagine the sound of what seemed like millions of bees? I suspect we were all feeling completely intimidated and slightly terrified, but the men certainly weren't showing it. Of course, I was suited and booted, but all I wanted to do was scratch my nose – not a chance of that happening!

We were all quite subdued, to say the least. When the instructor asked for a volunteer to lift a frame black with bees out of a hive, there were no initial takers. After a slightly uncomfortable silence, a voice from the back piped up, 'Ladies first!' Well, I had no other choice. So I took my first apprehensive steps towards that black cloud of bees – and that was me hooked. The men may have held back (and, interestingly, they all got stung), but I got in there, lost track of time and walked away with no stings, knowing that beekeeping was indeed for me. Thankfully, Eamonn shares my passion.

Beekeeping comes with certain expenses, however. The course shouldn't be too expensive but, if you want to keep bees, the initial outlay will be costly. I urge caution if you have been given an old hive to get started – at least with a new hive you can rest assured that it is disease free. I think practical experience is required before using pre-owned equipment or, indeed, attempting to make your own hives. Then there is the expense of your bee suit, not to mention your first colony of bees. A budget of between €400 and €500 should see you well set up. If it's something you really want to do, then make a list for your upcoming birthday or Christmas.

Remember, it takes years and years to become an experienced beekeeper. You'll have good years and bad years, just like life really. But with that experience comes a wealth of knowledge – and honey, lots and lots of delicious honey.

GEESE

You may have wondered why I didn't include geese with rearing chickens and turkeys for the table. This is what happens when

you name your animals, folks! We could never consider eating Mahatma Gander, Willow Goose or any of their offspring. It's simply not for us. However, if you decide to keep geese, be sure to have plenty of grass for them, as they spend most of their days eating it. And, just like ducks, they need plenty of water. Geese are easily reared for the table but, again, like ducks, they are more difficult to pluck than chickens. Because geese eat so much grass, the yolks of their eggs are the most vibrant yellow colour.

Try a goose-egg omelette for something different – you'll only need one egg to feed the entire family.

IT'S A BIG STEP, SO ENJOY IT

Whatever you decide to rear, it's important to enjoy the experience. Like everything in life, the more you put into something, the more you get out of it. If time is a real issue for you at the moment, then rearing animals is not for you. But you never know what's around the corner, and there's no doubt that the quality of food you rear yourself will be second to none.

If this is something that's been at the back of your mind for some time, think it through fully and then go for it – you won't look back!

Gifts from Nature

8

🍎 FORAGING FOR FOOD 🍎

AS MUCH AS I LOVE the arrival of spring, bringing with it the promise of fluffy chicks and an abundance of food in the garden, I find there is something truly magical about the onset of autumn. The falling leaves carpet the ground in glorious hues of gold, orange and brown, and who can resist piling them up and kicking them? Those leaves have the uncanny knack of releasing the inner child in even the most sensible person. But as the temperatures drop and nature begins its hibernation, there's still plenty of food to be found. This is an excellent opportunity to get all the family out into the fresh air for a walk in the countryside.

Foraging, at any time of the year, is such an exciting part of sustainable living, and rarely costs anything more than time and enthusiasm. The goodness of a bowl of nettle soup is not to be underestimated. The health benefits of rosehip syrup are well documented and, in times past, when citrus fruits were scarce, rosehips provided many a child in Ireland with a much needed vitamin C boost.

I'm by no means an expert forager. To this day, I don't pick mushrooms unless I'm with someone with a lot of experience. Why take unnecessary risks? If you're not sure, don't eat it. But I'm guessing you know what nettles look like? And dandelions? And if you pass wild garlic in the spring, you'll be in no doubt of what you've found because of the wonderful smell.

In this chapter I'll cover a few basics that will get you out in the fresh air looking for some free food.

> Try to stay away from busy roads when you are foraging – not only will the fruit be polluted, but the traffic can be dangerous, especially with young children.

WILD STRAWBERRIES AND BLACKBERRIES

There are still areas in the countryside that run red with the most fantastic wild strawberries during the summer. They are usually closely guarded secrets though, and, while I've heard of some in my area, I've yet to find them. If you were lucky enough to find an abundance of ripe strawberries on your walk, would you be reluctant to reveal where they were? I suspect you might, but if you don't get out there and look, you'll never find these hidden gems.

Blackberries, on the other hand, are much more abundant. In good years, there's no end to the supply of these delicious berries. Blackberry jam doesn't have a long shelf-life, so remember to freeze some berries so that you can make fresh jam during the year. Freeze blackberries the same way as you would raspberries (see page 92).

THE BLACKTHORN

You will find blackthorn bushes growing wild in hedgerows and woodlands all over Ireland. The blackthorn produces a most beautiful white flower in March/April. This flower is edible and makes a very pretty addition to salads. In the autumn, sloes appear on the bushes. Now, beware, the blackthorn is a very prickly bush, so picking sloes is a delicate operation. Sloes, which are a blue-black colour, are a very bitter fruit and certainly not one that you'll pick from the bush and eat. But they do make wonderful jellies and, of course, sloe gin (see recipe on page 128).

You may already know that the wood from the blackthorn makes the sturdiest of walking sticks. They are prized worldwide because of their lovely knotted features. I usually wait until after the first frost to collect sloes. I then freeze them and use what I need to make sloe gin and sloe vodka for Christmas.

ROSEHIPS

Rosehips, the fruit of the wild rose, are found in hedgerows and ditches all over Ireland. The vibrant orange/red hips brighten up the countryside every autumn. Rosehips are not a fruit to be eaten raw. Use them to make a syrup (see recipe on page 117) and you'll be armed with the finest vitamin C boost to see you through the winter. I don't pick rosehips until after the first frost, as the frost make the insides of the hip softer and the flavour develops more.

DANDELIONS

Who doesn't recognise the 'pissy bed'? What child didn't think that if you picked dandelions you would wet the bed? The fact is, the dandelion is a natural diuretic, so there was some truth to the old saying.

You don't have to go to hedgerows in the countryside to find dandelions. I'm sure you are only too familiar with them in your garden. But have you ever thought about eating them? Well, there's lots you can do with them. To start off, why not consider adding the wonderfully vibrant yellow petals to your salad bowl? The leaves are also edible, and the young leaves are perfect for a salad. The older leaves can be a little bitter so, instead of using them for salads, wilt them like spinach leaves. And you can always enjoy a cup of dandelion tea (put washed leaves in a teapot, cover them in boiling water and allow to brew for a few minutes). It's great for the old water retention.

NETTLES

Nettles are as instantly recognisable as dandelions. Neglect your garden for any length of time and you'll know all about them. Who among us escaped childhood without dozens of nettle stings throughout the summer months? Even now, when Eamonn and I make our way to our beehives, I'm on full alert for those pesky weeds. So, why on earth would I consider eating them? They make a truly delicious peppery flavoured soup that's packed with vitamin C – and it's free! I still laugh when I recall the first time I made it. My poor daughter Kate was convinced she was going to be stung as she sipped her soup. But, have no fear, the sting is completely removed by cooking. If you are making nettle soup for children, I recommend liquidizing it really well. Arm yourself with rubber gloves to pick nettles and pick only the young leaves on the top of the plants to get the best-flavoured leaves. Experiment with nettles – add them to pasta or make nettle tea. It's free, so why not give it a go?

CRAB APPLES

This is one for the crab-apple jelly enthusiasts. Wild crab-apple trees can be found all over the countryside, and the older the tree, the bigger the crop. Don't think for one second that you'll enjoy a snack on some crab apples as you walk through the countryside. Oh my, they are bitter! But they just sing when you add water and sugar to make crab-apple jelly. If you are making some, try adding flavours like cinnamon or chilli for something different.

Whether you decide to forage for blackberries or use some back-garden nettles for soup, you are receiving a gift from nature and using it to nourish your family. How did it happen that today we are more comfortable using food that is suffocating in plastic packaging than we are picking it fresh from the ground? Like I said, I'm not an expert forager, but every year I find more and more gifts that nature bestows upon me.

> Remember to only take what you need. Don't strip bushes of their fruit or flowers. It's important to share with nature, so leave plenty for birds, bees and insects to have their fill too.

THE HEALING POWER OF FOOD

HONEY

Some of the foods in my garden are as healing as they are nourishing. The prime example is our honey. The healing properties of honey are well documented, but before I started growing my own food I thought that honey was just for eating. Nowadays, I call it my number-one superfood. A sore throat doesn't stand a chance against our honey. It's antibiotic and antiseptic qualities are powerful. If Ruth cuts her knee, I wash it and dab honey on it. Cuts, colds, burns, sores – I rely on honey for all these common ailments. And not just for my family. If I

think any of the chickens are under the weather, I add honey to their drinkers. It works a treat. And then there's hayfever. Our bees travel a distance of approximately three miles, bringing back pollen from all the fields and hedgerows in this area. By ingesting our honey, the children build up a resistance to local pollens that would usually trigger hayfever. Whether you suffer from hayfever or not, it's well worth trying to find a local honey producer in your area.

GARLIC

The healing powers of garlic, particularly in relation to the respiratory system, are also well documented. We are fortunate not to be prone to coughs and colds in this house, but if there is a sign of one extra garlic is included in meals immediately.

Poultry keepers take note: garlic works brilliantly for your chickens too. One of the biggest problems with chickens at the moment is respiratory infections. I find adding garlic to their drinkers boosts their immune systems and guards against respiratory problems. And I can't forget the wonderful home-made garlic spray that protects my plants from the likes of greenflies.

ROSEHIP SYRUP

When I make rosehip syrup for the kitchen, I also make some for the garden, specifically for the chickens. If it's good enough for us, then it's good enough for them. I guess it's easy to see why I not only have healthy children but also an exceptionally healthy flock of chickens. I don't spend any money on vitamin boosts for either my children or my poultry. I'm just going back to basics and working with nature.

Epilogue

I'M NOT A PROFESSIONAL CHEF. I'm not a horticulturist. I'm not a professional photographer. I'm not a farmer. I was the girl who could burn water, and I truly believed that my fingers might be any colour throughout my life, but they would never be green. I had never seen a pig or a chicken up close. Wasps and bees were all the same to me – to be avoided at all costs.

Thanks to my parents, however, I knew what good food was. Because of my dad's vegetable garden, I appreciated the goodness of home-grown potatoes and vegetables. But that was my dad's hobby and, as I'm the stamp of my mother, I just presumed I had missed out on those 'grow your own' genes. And that was fine with me. But life is funny, and you never know what's around the corner.

Well, that girl who could burn water went around that corner. I am now a certified trainer, sharing my knowledge and skills with those who want to know more about growing food. I blog, I write and I broadcast about the realities of growing food. About a life that is simple but full of riches. And I am having the time of my life.

I've tried to keep this book to the basics. I wanted to share some of my ideas with you so that you too could start on your own self-sufficient path without being overwhelmed at the thought of what might lie ahead. Believe me, though, what lies ahead is really wonderful. Like everything in life, take it one step at a time and try to enjoy the process. Try not to get overwhelmed and stressed along the way. At any point if I start to feel like this, I step away and remind myself of why I do this. It's as much about being happy and content as it is about growing good food. From the day I started on this road I promised myself that the one thing I would not die from was stress. And I am keeping this promise to myself – not just for me, but for my family.

This way of life started with collecting eggs and sowing seeds. Nowadays, it's so much more. It's about home-made tomato sauces, parsley pestos, smoking cheese, making yoghurt and discovering more and more free foods in the surrounding fields and hedgerows. It's about choosing new flavours for our sausages, preserving fruit and drying herbs. And all the while, we're spending less and less money on groceries every week.

People attending my classes to learn about keeping chickens are often really worried about things going wrong, and I completely understand that. They ponder on whether their chickens should have check-ups at the vet's clinic or whether they should heat their coops. I can see that even before they get their chickens they are stressing. Here's what I tell them: Throw your mind back to your grandparents' time. If you drove into any yard in the countryside, chickens would scatter in all directions upon your arrival. Did backyard poultry keepers of our grandparents' era worry about worming and vaccinating their chickens? Did they buy brand new coops for their flock? The answer is very likely to be 'no', but they managed to have healthy, happy chickens. Of course, I'm not saying you shouldn't care about the welfare of your animals, but don't fret either. After all, chickens are tough little cookies, and the fact that you care so much will see you through most situations.

Finally, throughout this book my intention has never been to tell you what to do or how to live your life. I'm just sharing my story – well, our story. The story of Eamonn, Fiona, Joe, Kate, Ellie and Ruth – a regular family, eating good food every day.

By pointing out how I started this journey with no experience, I'm not looking for you to say, 'Wow, you really are great.' I want you to think, 'If Fiona can do it, so can I!'

And, trust me, you can.

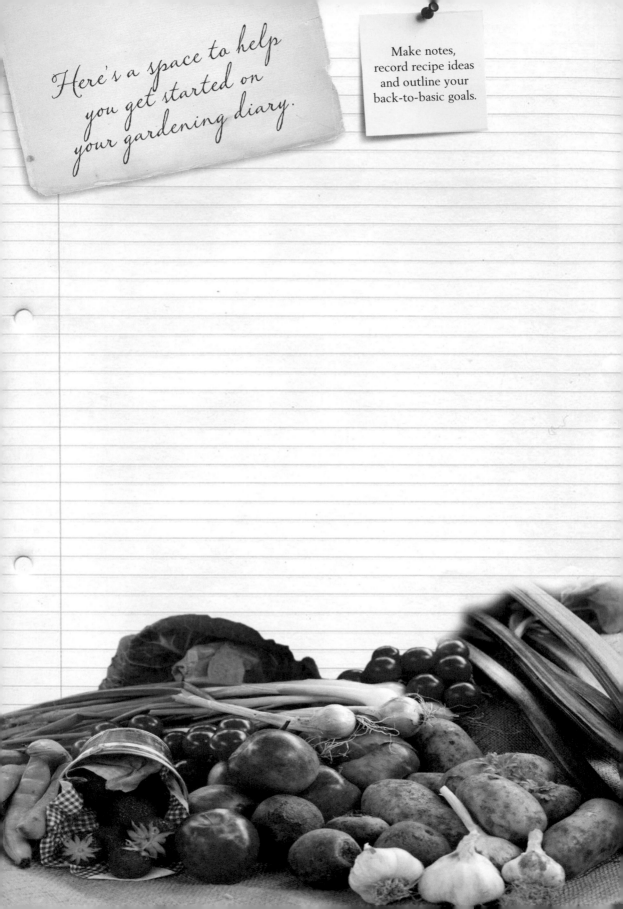

Here's a space to help you get started on your gardening diary.

Make notes, record recipe ideas and outline your back-to-basic goals.